CONTENTS

INTRO	Let the Magic Begin!	
SECTION ONE	**SAVING BIG AT DISNEY WORLD**	
ONE	Planning Ahead for Big Savings	11
TWO	Disney Lodging & Travel Tips	17
THREE	Free Fun at Disney Resorts	29
FOUR	Walkways and Nature Trails	45
FIVE	Free Fun at Disney Springs	51
SIX	Free Fun at Disney's Boardwalk	55
SEVEN	Disney Transportation Fun	59
EIGHT	Disney's Town of Celebration	63
NINE	Dining Tips To Eat Well & Save Big	67
SECTION TWO	**PREPARING FOR YOUR DISNEY VACATION**	
TEN	When To Go? Where To Stay?	81
ELEVEN	Making Dining Reservations	93
TWELVE	Disney Meal Plans	97
THIRTEEN	Disney Fast Passes	103
FOURTEEN	Disney Daily Guide Maps	109
FIFTEEN	Our Top 10 Disney Dining Locations	127

	SECTION THREE	DISNEY DAILY GUIDE MAPS	
SIXTEEN		Everything You Need To Know About Disney Daily Guide Maps	139
SEVENTEEN		The Magic Kingdom	145
		Magic Kingdom Daily Guide Map	155
EIGHTEEN		Hollywood Studios	185
		Hollywood Studios Daily Guide Map	197
NINTEEN		Epcot	219
		Epcot Daily Guide Map	229
TWENTY		Animal Kingdom	253
		Animal Kingdom Daily Guide Map	263

CLOSING THOUGHTS - IS DISNEY THE SECRET TO A HAPPY FAMILY?

INTRODUCTION

LET THE MAGIC BEGIN!

Hello, my name is Chuck. My wife and I have been taking our 4 children to Disney World for over 20 years. I still remember our first trip to Disney World when my oldest daughter, Abby, was three years old. My wife, Tara, and I decided to visit the Magic Kingdom because we thought that Abby would enjoy the wonder and fantasy of the Disney characters and, of course, the Cinderella castle.

I really wasn't expecting that there would be much at Disney World that would be of interest to a "mature" adult like me – but, of course, I was wrong. Once I relaxed a bit and allowed myself to act like a kid again, the magic of Disney began to capture me as well.

It didn't take long before I was caught up in the fantasy of this wonderful place "where dreams come true." Somehow, I found myself wide-eyed and mystified by the wonder of magical fairies and super friendly life size mice. Maybe it was the pixie dust, maybe it was the excessive sugar in giant waffle cone ice-cream bowl I had just eaten, but I was hooked along with all the other children, young and old alike.

I knew it was time to come home when I found myself a little misty-eyed during the coronation ceremony for Cinderella and prince Charming – Enough is enough. Still, we have returned to this dreamy place with our four daughters many times since that day. Since the birth of

READY. SET. DISNEY

our oldest daughter, who is now in her twenties, our family has taken multiple yearly trips to Disney World in pursuit of magic and adventure. It has been an education in stretching our collective creative and imaginative energy. Just as Disney has been a place of bonding and connection for our family, we hope that it will become such a place for your family as well.

Though our initial Disney experience was a positive one, we have come to realize that not everyone has the same magical mouse encounter on their first trip to Disney World. There have been occasions over the years when we too have had less than wonderful Disney adventures. We have discovered that the magic is not automatic.

Enjoying your Disney vacation will be much easier if you are fully prepared for the adventure that awaits you. It is our hope that this booklet will help, in some capacity, with this process and will give you an opportunity to have a super amazing Disney vacation – even on the first try.

We believe there are certain tips and, somewhat, "secret" tricks that can help increase the possibility for a successful Disney experience. Preparing in advance for your Disney trip will greatly increase the odds that your vacation will be a magical adventure. It is our desire to help you experience the magic and discover why so many families call Disney World "the happiest place on earth."

We know that so much has been written on the topic of Disney World. Navigating the myriad of websites and forums can be a daunting task. That's why we wanted to make this booklet easy to read and practical. Rather than load you down with endless details and overload your brain, we have worked hard to make this book readable, practical and helpful.

This book, along with our was written because we have learned just about everything there is to know about Disney over the years (much of it by making mistakes) and we truly want to help families to enjoy their first Disney experience as we did so many years ago.

This book is intended to get you started with the process of planning and preparing for your trip to Disney World without overwhelming you with insignificant information. We have 3 goals for you as you read through this book,

1) That you will discover ways to plan and prepare for a magical vacation that will allow you to relax and enjoy every moment with your loved ones once you finally enter each Disney park.

2) That you will learn enough from the many lessons we have discovered through our years of Disney experience to help make your Disney vacation as magical as possible.

3) That you will discover the many ways to experience Disney World outside of the Disney parks. This will not only allow you to experience aspects of Disney that many never do but will also provide alternatives to experiencing the Disney magic without breaking your budget.

We are so excited for the adventure that awaits you and your loved ones. Let's Go To Disney World!

READY. SET. DISNEY

SECTION ONE

Saving Big At Disney World

READY. SET. DISNEY

ONE

PLANNING
AHEAD FOR BIG SAVINGS

Planning a trip to Disney World can be a daunting task for anyone, especially if you don't have any idea where to begin.

If you are still early in the planning process and have several months before your departure date, there are several tips and tricks we have learned that may help you in your preparation.

On the other hand, if you are leaving tomorrow, don't worry, keep reading, there is still plenty packed into this booklet that will be of help to you in your process.

There are several ways to reduce the cost of your trip to Disney World through planning and a little preparation.

This section is designed to help assist you in considering cost effective ways of planning your Disney trip. With a little foresight, we believe you can save big and still have a Magical adventure. Here are several tips to consider as you prepare...

READY. SET. DISNEY

Save A Little Each Week

Though it may seem trivial and obvious, you can usually lighten the blow of the cost of your Disney vacation by saving a little bit over a longer time-period.
We have often designated a Disney jar or box for loose change or for money we received unexpectedly throughout the year.

Looking forward to a Disney vacation can be just the incentive to save elsewhere. Taking the money that you save from using a coupon or from skipping your morning Starbucks coffee could add up throughout the year. If the suggestion of skipping your morning Starbucks just caused steam to come out of your ears, maybe you can come up with an alternative idea.

Regardless, the Disney jar can be a visible-tangible reminder of a future magical adventure. The jar can also be a great way to dream with your children and give them an opportunity to help make the family Disney trip a reality.

Bring Along Commonly Used Items

There are certain items that you might consider bringing to Disney rather than purchasing them  on your trip since most things will be much more expensive on Disney property. Some of the items you might consider bringing along are sunglasses, hats, water bottles, baby supplies, back packs, rain ponchos, trading pins to trade with Disney workers, sunscreen, autograph books and pens, glow sticks and disposable cameras. You can usually buy glow in the dark sticks, bracelets and necklaces very inexpensively at your local dollar store before your trip. Why not buy extra and have your kids share them with others during the firework show? It will add to the fun!

You might also consider bringing your favorite snacks and drinks as well. Let's face it, our kids love snacks and you will likely purchase them eventually; why not save a little cash by purchasing them before you leave or outside of the park when you arrive?

Bringing snacks along with you will likely save you money on snacks in the long run. You can still splurge on a snack or two at the park in your weak moments if you so choose.

Many of these items can also be ordered on Amazon Pantry and delivered directly to your room for much less than you would be able to purchase similar items at Disney. Planning ahead and ordering online can save you some money and stress.

Pin Trading

If your little one wants to get involved with pin trading with Disney cast members, there is a less expensive way to get started. Pin necklaces can be purchased online through E-bay or at many Walmart, Target or other department stores.

READY. SET. DISNEY

Your child can purchase pins online or at a local department store and then trade them with cast members throughout the parks. You can buy trading pins much cheaper than buying the pins at Disney. Just make sure the pins are legitimate Disney pins before you purchase them, otherwise, you may not be permitted to trade them with the Disney workers.

Bring Your Own Stroller

Although bringing your own stroller might be a pain and may cost you an additional airline fee, you might want to do the math before you make your final decision. When you figure in the cost of renting a stroller for each day of your vacation, it might just pay off to pay the airline baggage fee to bring your own stroller from home.

Stroller rental in the parks is currently around $20 per day and the Disney Stroller you rent will likely have less bells and whistles than your own stroller from home. Bringing your own stroller may save you money and be more personable to the needs of your family.

Bring Strollers For Older Children

One thing that we realized through the years was the value of having a stroller available for our older children during the longer days at the parks. We discovered that having a stroller was a nice luxury when our kids got tired or when we had a ton to carry around the park.

We used a stroller for our kids even when they were plenty old enough to walk on their own. Giving each of our kids the opportunity to ride in a stroller instead of walking from time to time made everyone a little less cranky later in the day. Also, strollers provide extra space to store jackets, snacks and drinks that will come in handy throughout the day.

More On Strollers & Pack and Plays

There are locations outside of Disney World property that rent strollers more reasonably for multiple days or by the week. If you need an alternative to renting a stroller from Disney, you may want to look into renting off Disney property. It's a little inconvenient at the outset, but it may be worth the effort.

If you are concerned about having enough room to bring along a pack n play for your infant or toddler, no worries, Disney provides pack n plays free of charge to families; Just ask the concierge at check in or call guest services from your room phone.

Purchase Gift Cards

Purchasing Disney gift cards throughout the year allows you to spread the cost of your trip out over a longer period of time and reduces the burden of having to pay for the trip all at one time. Giving your child a Disney Gift Card to

READY. SET. DISNEY

carry with them is a creative way to give them spending money without giving them cash or your credit card. This  will give younger children a sense of freedom and the opportunity to manage their own budget for the trip. Also, sites like Raise.com, Ebay, Card Granny and Sam's Club often offer gift cards at a discount of their face value. Purchasing gift cards in advance of your trip might allow you to save money while also giving you the opportunity to pay for your trip a little bit at a time.

Sign Up For A Disney Visa Card

Though it may not be the best option for every person,  signing up for a Disney Visa card comes with certain perks and provides for discounts throughout Disney World which can help reduce the over-all cost of your Vacation. Also, Disney card offers often come with 6 months interest free credit.

We are not advising that you to go into debt to pay for your Disney vacation, However, if you have the money to pay the card off after your trip, you will likely save a good bit by using it during your vacation.

TWO

DISNEY LODGING AND TRAVEL TIPS

The questions we most hear from families who are preparing to make their Disney reservations is "Should we book our tickets and room together in a package or should we make separate room and ticket reservations." The answer to that question depends on several factors.

<u>Are you flying to Disney?</u> If you fly to Disney it is likely that you will be staying on Disney property. In general, staying just outside of Disney property is a bit cheaper.

However, staying on Disney property prevents you from needing to rent a car or from having to find alternative transportation to the parks. Also, staying on Disney property allows you to get the "full" Disney experience.

<u>How early are you booking</u>? Prices go up for Disney reservations the closer you are to your arrival date. This is simply the law of supply and demand – so book early if possible. The closer you are to departure when you make your reservations, the more you will likely save by staying off Disney property.

<u>Do you want the meal plan</u>? Disney does not allow guests to include the meal plan without booking your entire trip as a package. We give you some of our thoughts on the meal plan in the Dining Tips section below. We have done

READY. SET. DISNEY

Disney many times with and without the meal plan and have discovered ways to eat great either way.

In general, the meal plan is great but expensive, so unless you are able to score the free meal plan that is sometimes offered in the fall you may wish to pass on the meal plan. If you choose to bypass the meal plan, you may do better to book your room and tickets separately. We give some advice on how to book tickets and room separately below.

Consider Traveling During A Low Season

Though you may not have the flexibility to do so, traveling to Disney World during one of their low seasons will save you money and enhance your overall experience. We have noticed a drastic difference in the level of our enjoyment of Disney World depending solely on the season.

Our best times have almost always been during a low season. Of course, if your only choice is to go during one of the busy seasons, don't be discouraged, the magic will still be there amidst the crowds. With a little planning you can have a great time – even when its packed. Planning ahead will be especially important if you are traveling during one of the high seasons.

We have traveled extensively to Disney in times of both high and lower attendance; traveling in low season is absolutely the way to go. Not only are the lines shorter and restaurants easier to book, Disney hotels and vacation packages are typically 20 to 30% cheaper during the low seasons.

Low Season Dates - Regarding the chart below, note that, historically, the least busy days at Disney World are in the winter and Fall. There are peaks during the holidays and spring break.

Overall, the month of September, late November and early December are the least busy seasons followed by January, early February and early November. **We have found late February and early March to be fairly tolerable as well.**

This pattern is generally consistent from year to year though it is important that you are aware of special events (i.e. marathons, specialty days etc.) Special events will typically cause the parks to swell even during a low season.

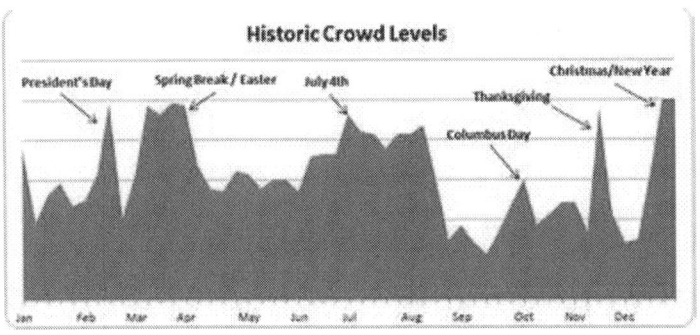

Note also that weekends are generally much busier than weekdays. Fridays through the day are typically less busy than Friday evenings. Friday evenings and Saturdays are usually the busiest times of the week to visit the parks and Sundays are not much better.

If your trip to Disney will feature days of relaxation with less time within the parks on certain days, we recommend

that you choose the weekends to relax and explore and choose to go to the parks on the less busy weekdays.

Consider Extending Your Stay

Though an extended stay may not be a possibility for some, there are several advantages to staying at Disney for longer periods of time.

First, the price of Disney tickets is heavily weighted over the first few days. The longer you stay, the lower the per day cost of each ticket.

For example, the price for a 10-day ticket is currently only $30 more than the 7-day ticket. That's only $10 per ticket per day for an additional 3 days of Disney fun. The following chart shows 1 to 10-day ticket prices.

Number of Days	Adult	Price to Add Day	Child	Price to Add Day
1 (Magic Kingdom)	105.44	n/a	99.05	n/a
1 (Animal Kingdom, Epcot, Hollywood Studios)	101.11	n/a	93.72	n/a
2	200.22	94.78	186.38	87.33
3	291.81	91.59	271.58	85.20
4	313.11	21.30	291.81	20.23
5	323.76	10.65	302.46	10.65
6	334.41	10.65	313.11	10.65
7	345.06	10.65	323.76	10.65
8	355.71	10.65	334.41	10.65
9	366.36	10.65	345.06	10.65
10	377.01	10.65	355.71	10.65

Also, staying longer by adding a few days to your trip will allow you to relax a bit more, not trying to cram everything into each day. Rotating days at the park with relaxing days by the pool can be a great way to add variety and enhance your entire vacation. When you have a few extra days, you will find yourself avoiding the busiest times, relaxing by the pool, enjoying your family and heading to the parks when the craziness dies down.

If you can extend your stay from 5 or 7 days to 9 or 10, each day will be less crazy and more enjoyable. Perhaps some of the money saving ideas in this guide will help you save enough in other areas to make this a reality.

Take A Pass On The Hopper Pass

Unless you are only planning to be at Disney for a few days and want to visit multiple parks in a brief period of time,  we recommend that you skip the hopper pass. If your time is limited and you want to see as much as possible in a short time, then the hopper pass may make sense for your family.

However, there is so much to see and experience within each park that we have found it best to plan your entire day around only one park if possible. This way you spend more time enjoying your day and less time on Disney transportation traveling between parks.

Similar to the park ticket itself, the per day cost of adding the hopper pass decreases as you add additional days to your base ticket. This means that the Hopper pass makes more sense the longer you plan to visit Disney.
The hopper pass adds value, but it also adds expense and unnecessary travel time between the parks. On a really

READY. SET. DISNEY

busy day, it can take up to two hours to hop from one park to another.

Buy Discount Tickets

If you choose to purchase your ticket and accommodation separately, you can take advantage of both room only discounts and discount park ticket pricing. Check mousesavers.com for lots of great Disney information, including updates on current room only discounts. Once you have found a discount code, you can call Big Cheese Travel at 407.900.0185 or call Disney directly at (407) 939-1284 and present the code to the representative over the phone.

If you can't find a code, you should still ask the Disney representative if there is a "room only" discount available for your dates of travel. If you book at least a few months in advance there are typically room only discounts available.

For the lower than gate pricing on theme park tickets we recommend undercovertourist.com. The prices here are the lowest non-promotional rates that we have found on park tickets anywhere. Typically, families can save somewhere between 7 and 10% off the gate price by ordering through their website. It may be worth your time if you are not considering a Magic Your Way vacation package. We have gotten our tickets from time to time through UT, it may be worth the hassle of ordering your tickets in advance if you aren't planning on staying on Disney property.

Should I Wait Until My Kids Are Older?

We often hear families say they are planning to wait until their children are older to visit Disney World. The reasoning is that their kids are too small to enjoy the parks. However, we discovered that some of our favorite moments as a couple occurred at Disney while our kids were very small.

Disney offers so much for adults / parents; there is no need to wait before you start enjoying the parks. As the kids grew older, we focused more on things they would enjoy and missed some of the things we enjoyed when they were small.

Also, children under age 3 are free admission to Disney World so why wait until you have to pay for them before you decide to go? Just a thought...

Reduce Your Lodging Costs

The least expensive way to stay on Disney property is to bring your own tent and stay at Disney's Fort Wilderness campground. If creating great memories with your loved ones is your primary goal, why not create them by camping out with them - Disney style. There are also full hookup RV sites at the campground for those who want to drive their accommodations to Disney.

With campfires every night, character meet and greets and multiple trails to explore, this could be the perfect family adventure; and starting around $60 per night for tent sites and $100 for RV sites, the price is right. Of course, as with all Disney accommodations, the price goes up during busy

READY. SET. DISNEY

season. You can choose from a variety of camping experiences ranging from fully equipped cabins (kind of expensive but roomy) or full hook up RV sites to simple tent camping sites.

If camping is just not your thing, Disney has several great value resorts that won't break the budget. Our favorites are Disney's Art of Animation and the All-Star Music / Sports resorts.

If you are willing to stay off Disney property, lodging is typically cheaper, and you can take advantage of savings on breakfast if the hotel offers a free continental breakfast. Once again, prices will be cheaper everywhere during low seasons.

There are also a good number of hotel chains close to Disney that participate in Disney's "Good Neighbor Hotels" program. Booking at one of these hotels will not necessarily save you money, but it will likely assure you that the hotel meets certain quality and service standards set by Disney World. There are many resorts just off Disney property that offer accommodations on par with Disney. You can typically rent a one or two-bedroom condo at one of these resorts for a reasonable price. Be careful though, if you are getting a really good deal it's likely that you are being targeted for a timeshare tour.

If you are willing to endure the hassle of sitting through a "90-minute" time share presentation you can typically stay at some of these resorts at a discounted rate.

If you have a larger travel party, it may pay off to rent a home from a private owner and drive a few miles to Disney. One site that we have used with great success over the years is VRBO.com

Rent DVC Points

A little-known method of staying at a super nice Disney resort for less is to rent points from a Disney Vacation Club owner. It is not uncommon to save as much as 50% on some of Disney's most luxurious timeshare ownership properties. You can find out more about DVC and rent points at mouseownersforum.com. Another option that is a little easier but a little more expensive is to rent points through David's Vacation Club.

Big Cheese Travel

One major reason we have written this book is to help families to experience the magic and joy of Disney World just as our family has over the past 20+ years. We have learned many valuable lessons that we believe can help other families plan for and save at Disney World as well.

Over the years, we have given advice to tons of families based on the lessons we have learned from over a hundred trips to the parks. We have also, developed an "approach" to each Disney park that we believe will make your Disney vacation less frustrating and more fulfilling.

We have outlined our approach to each Disney park in 4 easy to follow guide maps, one for each Disney park. We will discuss the Disney Daily Guide Maps more beginning in

READY. SET. DISNEY

Chapter 16. You can jump ahead to The Guide Maps for each park in chapters 17-20..

Take A Road Trip

If you have more than 2 or 3 people traveling in your party, it may be a good idea to drive to Disney World rather than fly. Our family of 6 has driven to Disney World every year for over 20 years. Though we have had opportunity to fly, there are many reasons that we have chosen to drive instead.

Over the years, we have saved thousands in air fare, created countless family memories, and have had the freedom of personal transportation to explore the endless World of Disney once we arrived.

Though Disney is very good at moving a lot of people from place to place, nothing compares to having your own transportation while at Disney. If you have multiple drivers and are planning to be at Disney longer than a few days, it might make sense to drive.

Also consider that many Disney locations are difficult to get to quickly through Disney transportation. Hopping from resort to resort or visiting a nice restaurant outside of Disney can be a bit of a pain without your own mode of transportation.

Also, some of the best dining experiences and shows at Disney are not in the parks but at the various Disney resorts. Though you can get to these locations via Disney transportation, you may need to take multiple transfers to arrive at your destination.

Orlando is loaded with many great restaurants and shopping locations. We often like to eat at some of these very nice dining locations just off Disney property from when we have the opportunity. Though Disney will take you to any dining location on Disney property, they will not take you to a location outside of Disney property.

If you do not have a vehicle while at Disney and need transportation to a location off Disney property, we recommend using Uber rather than renting a taxi. We have found that Uber is typically faster and less expensive than other alternatives in the Orlando area.

Invite The Grandparents

I'm sure this one made a few of you laugh out loud. But let's face it, grandparents usually have a good bit of expendable income, lots of time and love their grandkids. Inviting the grand parents on your Disney vacation may be a great decision for the whole family. Plus, if your grandparents happen to live in Florida, they may be able to get special ticket pricing and Florida resident discounts…Bonus!

READY. SET. DISNEY

THREE

FREE FUN AT DISNEY RESORTS

It is not necessary to enter one of the Disney theme-parks to have a great time at Disney World. We have found that the Disney deluxe, moderate and value resorts have a lot to offer.

Each Disney resort is especially themed with tons to see and experience. If you take some time out of your schedule to explore the Disney resorts, you will not be disappointed.

You can take Disney transportation from any of the four theme parks to any of the resort hotels. If you drive to one of the resorts, you can get a FREE 3-hour parking permit from the gate attendant. Some resorts do not require a permit, just tell them you want to grab a snack or take a look around.

The only resorts that may not allow you to park during the busier seasons are The Polynesian resort, The Grand Floridian resort and the resorts on the Boardwalk. However, each of these resorts are accessible through Free Disney transportation.

We have discovered that it has become a little more difficult to park at the Caribbean Beach resort now that the Disney Skyliner has been finished and the Caribbean is the main hub for this new system. However, most resorts, including the Caribbean, will allow you to come in and stay

READY. SET. DISNEY

for a bit as long as you mention that you will be dining at the resort during your visit. So, it might be a good idea to plan on eating a meal at Old Port Royale or Sebastian's.

Disney Resort Pools

Each Disney resort pool is specifically themed to match the feel and atmosphere of the resort. For example, the main pool at the Coronado Springs resort looks like a Mayan ruin.

The Stormalong Bay pool at the Yacht & Beach Club

includes a huge "shipwreck" that contains a one of a kind waterslide and a beautiful tropical pool. The pool at the Wilderness Lodge starts as a spring in the lobby, passes under a bridge, then cascades down a waterfall into the pool and ends in a geyser that goes off once an hour! The "feel" of the pool is of a remote Canadian lake. The food in the food court is really good here as

well so you may want to plan lunch or dinner here when you visit – might I suggest the grilled chicken sandwich?

The pool at the Caribbean Beach resort has a pirate theme that is irresistible to most young aspiring pirates.

The pool area at the Animal Kingdom Lodge (a family favorite for our family) is nestled within the setting of an African savannah with views of Zebras, Giraffes, flamingos and other savannah animals. African music plays softly among the sights and sounds of the African savannah.

Though the Animal Kingdom lodge is a must see, it can be somewhat of a hassle getting there without a vehicle. Though it is close in proximity to the Animal Kingdom theme park, the Animal Kingdom Lodge is a bit further from the other theme parks. If you have several hours to kill, it is well worth the journey to get there.

READY. SET. DISNEY

Do You Prefer a Beach?

We love to hang out at one of the several beautiful beaches at the Caribbean Beach resort.
Rarely are any of these beaches crowded and there are

hammocks on each beach if you want to catch a nap or read a good book. If you are at the Caribbean Beach resort, we recommend taking an evening walk through the central Island or along the
promenade around the lake. This is a great walk for both couples and families. There are several benches spaced along the promenade where you may choose to stop and relax for a bit.

There are many peaceful and romantic places to sit on the island as well. There is also a very nice playground for little ones. Why not sip on a cold beverage and let the kids play while you soak in the beautiful scenery of the tropical island setting.

There is also a beach that runs between the Polynesian resort and the Grand Floridian resort that is rarely occupied after prime sun hours. This beach is a great location to relax or for the kids to build a sandcastle. This

is also a nice place for couples to enjoy a picnic or romantic conversation. If you time it right, this is also a great place to view the Magic Kingdom fireworks or the Electrical Water Pageant, its stunning!

Deluxe Resort Lobbies

The deluxe resort lobbies have a variety of incredible atmospheres that fit with the theme of each individual resort. Some lobbies, including the Grand Floridian, regularly have artists performing for hotel guests. Couples, why not take some time one evening to enjoy the elegant atmosphere within the Grand Floridian Resort Lobby? Just grab a cold (or hot) drink and a comfortable seat, and take in the sights and sounds of one of the nightly performers? The musicians performing nightly in the Grand Floridian lobby are world class and worth taking the time to see. It's relaxing, it's magical and it's free!

We also recommend that you take some time to explore the main lobby at the Animal Kingdom Lodge. The views of the savannah from the cable bridge in the main lobby are breathtaking. As you relax among the African décor, you

READY. SET. DISNEY

will be captured by the sights, sounds and smells of Africa. Be careful though, the smells wafting from the Boma may

tempt you beyond your ability to resist making dinner reservations. On many occasions we have taken a board game or a deck of cards and played games in the side room just off the main lobby, it's a wonderful atmosphere to play and have fun with family and friends.

The Polynesian Resort lobby and surrounding grounds are a tropical paradise. The atmosphere of the Polynesian

Islands surrounds you as you stroll along the tiki torch lit walkways. There is also a very nice gift shop off the lobby if you are looking for some souvenirs. The smell of authentic Polynesian food

fills your senses while sounds of a Hawaiian Luau echo in

the distance. Why not grab a Lapu Lapu from the bar at Ohana or a hot coffee from Captain Cook's and have a nice evening with someone special?

This is another family favorite. We love to grab some bread pudding from

Ohana (One of our favorite restaurants at Disney) or a pineapple ice cream cone and sit outside of Captain Hook's. It's quite amazing!

Evenings at the Polynesian Resort are especially magical because you are surrounded by tiki torch lit walkways and all the sights and sounds of Polynesia. The atmosphere is unbeatable.

Several of the resorts, including The Animal Kingdom Lodge, The Boardwalk Inn, The Wilderness Lodge, The Grand Floridian, and The Yacht Club, offer FREE tours that are open to any Disney resort guest (whether you are staying at that resort or not).

Some of the tours require a reservation, so inquire in advance. If you prefer to take your own tour, you might consider asking the concierge at each resort to provide you with a resort map.

Moderate Resort Food Courts

Disney moderate resorts offer great food with creative theming to match. The food court at Port Orleans Riverside is beautifully reminiscent of old New Orleans.

The food courts at the newly renovated Caribbean Beach and Coronado Springs resorts offer a variety of food options along with the wonder of detail that is unmatched outside of Disney. Experience the feel of the Caribbean Islands as you walk down a tropical Island street or enjoy a

READY. SET. DISNEY

cold drink, Caribbean style. The Caribbean resort has been a family favorite over the years. It's a relaxing place to eat, take a walk or just sit and have a drink.

If you are more in the mood for a Mexican adventure, you may want to take a brief siesta and enjoy some Mexican cuisine at the Coronado if that piques your interest.

With a little imagination, each meal at a Disney food court can become an amazing dining adventure. We recommend that you consider making the most of your mealtimes by planning your meal location ahead and setting aside enough time to enjoy each dining experience. We have found that many of our favorite memories were made when we slowed down our pace and really enjoyed our family meals together.

Value Resort Food Courts

The label of "value" resort might give off the impression that these resorts are of a lower quality. Some may assume that there is nothing to see or experience at these magical resorts; this is certainly not the case. There is still plenty of magic to be found at these resorts.

Each value resort is specially themed and designed to spark creativity and imagination. If you have little ones, the playground at Disney's Art of Animation is a must do.

Also, the food court at this resort has the greatest variety of breakfast and lunch options of any food court at Disney.

The All-Star Sports and All-Star Music Resorts offer  theming that is especially attractive to younger visitors and families. The All-Star Sports resort features gigantic versions of popular sports icons. Giant footballs, helmets, hockey sticks, etc. The grounds around each resort are huge sport fields or courts.

The All-Star Music resort has gigantic instruments and Piano shaped pool to add to its magical atmosphere and characteristic charm.

Taking some time to explore the variety and creativity of each Disney value resort is time well spent. If you're looking for a fun photo opportunity, consider visiting one of the All Star or Pop Century resorts. These hotels feature enormous "pop culture" icons that are great for family photos. You can choose to take

READY. SET. DISNEY

a family photo in front of a 35-foot Buzz Lightyear, a 30-foot football or a gigantic guitar.

Regardless of your hobby or interest, there will certainly be something that captures your attention at one of these value resorts. If you have young children, this might be a great way to spend some of your down time. We have spent many an afternoon exploring the various Disney resorts, it has become one of our favorite activities when visiting Disney.

Now that the Disney Skyliner is up and running, it's quite easy to travel between the Caribbean Beach Resort, the Pop Century Resort and Disney's Art of Animation. This is a wonderful way to spend an afternoon.

The Geyser at Wilderness Lodge

At Wilderness Lodge, a geyser (kind of a mini version of Old Faithful) spouts on the hour from 7:00 am to 10:00 pm. The geyser is located at the back of the property, past the pool. During the day, you can explore the woods from the Wilderness Lodge all the way to Fort Wilderness and back. If you stick around until dusk, you can stay to watch the lakeside movie shown on an inflatable outdoor screen. As with most deluxe resorts, there is a marshmallow cookout before the movie starts as well.

A Scavenger Hunt at Grand Floridian

At the Grand Floridian resort kids can go on a scavenger hunt to discover characters hidden in the walls, floors and ceiling of the resort. You can pick up the clues from the Bell Captain in the lobby.

If the kids finish the hunt, they will receive an official certificate from the Bell Captain. There are similar scavenger hunts, arts and craft activities and special events throughout the week at each Disney resort.

Consult the lobby concierge at each resort to get information about the activities you would like to participate in.

Free Fun at Disney's Fort Wilderness

You can take a 25-minute evening Wagon ride around Fort Wilderness Campground currently for $13/adult, $9/child (ages 3-9). The wagon rides are offered nightly at 6:00 pm and 8:30 pm and depart from in front of Pioneer Hall. No reservations are taken — just show up and pay cash.

READY. SET. DISNEY

Sing around the campfire and watch a FREE Disney movie. The campfire program at Ft. Wilderness is open to all Walt Disney World resort guests. The campfire is held every evening, at around 7pm in the fall and winter and around 8pm in the spring and summer, near the Meadow Trading Post.

The program starts with a sing-along and a marshmallow roast. You can bring your own food or purchase it from the Chuckwagon, which sells S'more kits for around $10 (enough for about 4 people).

The Chuckwagon also offers additional food items like pizza and hot dogs. Chip and Dale often greet the guests and sign autographs. It's a wonderful wilderness adventure – Disney style.

After the campfire, a Disney movie is shown on a large outdoor screen. There is some seating available on bleachers and benches, or you can lay out a blanket or set up a few camp chairs of your own. It's all very relaxed and everyone is having a good time.

No reservations are necessary to attend — just show up and enjoy. There is a charge for the wagon rides, but the campfire and movie are free. It's a ton of fun for the whole family with little or no expense.

Sing Along and Camp Fire at Grand Floridian

A similar outdoor campfire and movie program is offered at Disney's Beach Club Resort and at Disney's Grand Floridian Resort. There is a campfire sing-along on the beach, followed by a Disney movie. The resort that you choose will depend upon the environment you prefer.

If you want to choose your location based on the movies that are being shown at each resort, you can call Disney info for a schedule. S'more kits that make enough for about 4 people are sold for about $10 at each location. Remember, no reservations are necessary — just show up. Cost: FREE to all Disney resort guests.

Sing Along at Port Orleans Riverside

Port Orleans-Riverside offers a seasonal "Campfire on de' Bayou" with stories and sing-alongs around a fire at the Ol' Man Island Fishin' Hole. It usually runs in the winter, from Halloween through sometime in March, and only a couple of nights a week (most recently, Sunday and Thursday), weather permitting. Call Disney Guest Services to check dates and times before you show up.

READY. SET. DISNEY

Tri-Circle Ranch at Fort Wilderness

Tri-Circle Ranch is the home of the draft horses used to pull the trolleys down Main Street USA at the Magic Kingdom. These horses are boarded at Ft. Wilderness Tri-Circle Ranch. There are quite a few different horses to see and pony rides for very small children from 10 am to 5 pm for a small fee.

There is FREE day parking at the ranch and there is transportation from the day guest parking to the farm area by special buses that run only in the "Settlement." Once again, contact Disney Guest Services to check dates and times before heading to the ranch.

Outdoor Movies at The Caribbean Beach Resort

Outdoor Disney movies are also shown on certain nights at the Caribbean Beach resort, the Wilderness Lodge and others. Disney information will be able to tell you when and where your favorite movies are playing.

There is a good bet that you can find a movie you want to see playing at one of the Disney resorts. Pack a cooler, pop some popcorn and arrive about 30 minutes before the movie is scheduled to begin.

This has been a favorite free activity for our family over the years. With the variety of movie offerings, we can usually find a movie we all enjoy.

Kids Programs at Disney Resorts

Investigate special kids' programs at your Disney resort hotel. Disney goes to great lengths to provide fun and entertainment for children both inside of the theme parks and throughout Disney properties. The Deluxe resorts usually have kids'

recreation programs such as coloring, crafts, pool games, Hidden Mickey searches, and storytelling at various times. Cost: FREE to all Disney guests.

Parking at Disney Resorts

Recently, Disney has started charging a fee for parking at the Disney resorts. However, this $20 fee (a little less for value resorts and a little more for deluxe resorts) only applies to overnight parking for those staying at the Disney resorts.

If you are wanting to visit a Disney resort and parking is available, you may park there for free during the day.

READY. SET. DISNEY

Some resorts will offer you a three-hour pass, others will not place limits on the duration of your stay.

During busy seasons, parking at Magic Kingdom resorts and the Boardwalk will be difficult to secure unless you have a reservation at one of the restaurants associated with the resort. Regardless, you can always park at Disney Springs for free and take Disney transportation to anywhere on Disney property.

FOUR

DISNEY WALKWAYS AND NATURE TRAILS

There are lovely walkways or nature trails around almost all the resorts at Disney World. At night you can wander along the Polynesian's beach and watch the Electrical Water Pageant and the fireworks over the Magic Kingdom.

Walk through the tiki-torchlit gardens between the Great Ceremonial House and the beach.

Whether you are enjoying time alone, with a loved one or with family, these walks will add many wonderful Disney memories to your trip.

The walkway between the Polynesian resort and The Grand Floridian resort is one of our favorite walkways at Disney. It is simply magical to walk along the waterfront

READY. SET. DISNEY

with views of the Cinderella Castle in the background. We especially enjoy this walk at dusk or in the evening.

Rarely is this walkway congested. In fact, there have been many evenings when we didn't pass another person walking from the Polynesian to the Grand Floridian.

Along the way you can stop at Disney's wedding pavilion. If there isn't a wedding going on, it is usually left unlocked for guests to explore. This is a great place to snap a few photos. Our favorite picture spot is on the lake behind the pavilion. You can take pictures under the arch with the Cinderella Castle in the background.

We also love to walk around the promenade at the Caribbean Beach resort at night. The lighted pathway is breathtakingly beautiful and romantic. If you need a break, you can stop at one of the beaches and relax for a few moments in one of the beach hammocks. There are also many benches or pool side tables to stop and relax at on your journey.

If you prefer, you may wish to grab a drink at Sabastian's or sit outside of Old Port Royale with a sweet snack. It's only a short stroll over on the promenade to the newly completed DVC Riviera Resort. The Riviera has many beautiful lakeside tables along the water that provide a relaxing and romantic atmosphere.

The Fireworks and Epcot Night Show

Watch the Magic Kingdom Fireworks from the Grand Floridian boat dock. Narcoossees restaurant is nearby and receives the audio soundtrack from the Magic Kingdom, so you can enjoy the fireworks synchronized to the music. There's a little bit of delay due to the distance, but it still works. Seeing the fireworks reflect off the lake is, well, simply Magical.

From the Boardwalk, meander up to the back gate of Epcot, or over to Disney's Hollywood Studios around closing time and enjoy the music and perhaps a glimpse of Illuminations or *Fantasmic!*. The bridge that goes over to the Swan and Dolphin sometimes has nice views at that time. The bridge is a relaxing place, away from the crowds, to take in **Epcot Forever,** the new nighttime fireworks show at the end of each Epcot day.

READY. SET. DISNEY

Animal Viewing @ AK Lodge

At the Animal Kingdom Lodge, you can walk out to the viewing areas and see the exotic African animals roaming free. At certain times of the day you can catch the animals feeding. You can often capture some great pictures of Giraffes, Zebras etc. up close.

Note that the largest number of animals come out around dusk — you might not see very many during the day. Additionally, at night a Disney cast member will be there for several hours with night vision glasses for very fun viewing of the animals that can otherwise not be seen in the dark.

Also, a super place to relax is in one of the rocking chairs over-looking the savannah. There are 2 viewing areas off the main lobby and smaller ones off the resort wings. My wife and I love to kick back with a good book and a cup of coffee while relaxing in these rockers. Our girls also enjoy playing cards or reading here as well. Add an ice cold drink or a dessert from the Mara and the whole experience is even more magical.

Visit a Butterfly Garden

Visit a Butterfly Garden (a patch of land planted to create a habitat that attracts butterflies) at one of the resorts. There are currently two that we know about: at the Contemporary Resort, the garden is located on the left side as you walk out the back of the lobby towards the pool and lake; and at Ft. Wilderness, there is a garden outside the Outpost. You can call the Gardening Hotline at (407) 938-3900 for more information regarding butterfly gardens.

Watch the Electrical Water Pageant

This floating parade is visible nightly, usually starting at 9 pm, from Disney's Magic Kingdom-area resort hotel docks and beaches. The pageant takes about an hour to move slowly around the lake, stopping at each resort in order: The Polynesian, The Grand Floridian, The Wilderness Lodge, The Ft. Wilderness and The Contemporary. This show is a must see and there are many locations around The Seven Seas Lagoon to take it in. It's a great way to end the evening.

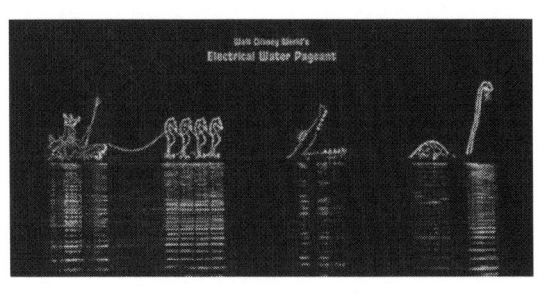

READY. SET. DISNEY

Disney's Wilderness Preserve

About 20 miles south of Orlando, at the headwaters of the Everglades ecosystem, is *The Nature Conservancy's Disney Wilderness Preserve.* Here you can observe native plants and animals by hiking a 2 1/2-mile trail. The Preserve is open 9:00 am – 5:00 pm daily (including weekends) November through March. It is closed on most holidays and closed on weekends March through October. Admission is FREE, though donations are appreciated. Before visiting, please call the preserve at (407) 935-0002 to verify that they are open.

FIVE

FREE FUN AT DISNEY SPRINGS

If you like to shop (or window shop), you'll enjoy this attractive shopping and restaurant zone, which also offers some great FREE entertainment. If you are staying on Disney property, you can use Disney transportation to get to Disney Springs. You can spend an entire day exploring the four unique neighborhoods of Disney Springs.

If you are staying at a Disney Spring resort area hotel, you can take the bus or walk. Otherwise, you'll probably need to drive or take a taxi. Parking is FREE. You will find countless eating and shopping opportunities with a variety of live entertainment around every corner.

You may wish to check out the wonderful interactive fountains where children (and adults who have the guts) enjoy playing and getting wet.

The new expansion also added an artificial spring, which is fun to wander around and explore. In the center of the main pool you can see a gentle

READY. SET. DISNEY

burbling which is supposed to be the actual location of the spring itself.

There's a cool functioning <u>Archimedes screw</u> which you can spin to pull water up out of the spring, plus fun little details built into the architecture and signage all around the spring itself. Check it out when you visit Disney Springs.

Check out some of the fanciful paintings of Disney Springs in years past that are displayed on the walls in the <u>Welcome Center</u>, which is the new Guest Relations booth for the Marketplace side of Disney Springs.

You can see the supposed "history" of Disney Springs, and the origins of the various buildings and features scattered around the area, all of which were fabricated out of whole cloth by the wizards at Disney Imagineering. The Welcome Center also has air conditioning, comfy chairs and FREE ice water.

The <u>Lego Imagination Center</u> has a FREE 3,000-square-foot outdoor play area filled with thousands of LEGO blocks, plus some amazing Lego sculptures for you to admire! Also, it normally participates in the Monthly Mini Model Build (usually first Tuesday of the month, starting at 5:00 pm), where kids ages 6-14 can build and take home a FREE mini model!

Ride on the Marketplace Carousel. The cost for this ride is only $3 per person. Children under 42 inches must be accompanied by an adult, but the adult is not required to pay. Great for the little ones.

There are multiple locations where individual musicians and bands perform in the evening, ranging from full-scale cover bands and dance bands to individual performers with just a guitar and microphone. Two places they usually show up are the small courtyard just next to the Boathouse, and the crossroads where the main walkway meets the walkway to the Orange parking garage. Entertainment is scheduled from about 7 PM to 11 PM (with breaks) most evenings during mid and high season and weekends during low season.

The House of Blues frequently offers **free live music** at its Front Porch Bar – enjoy for the cost of a drink! (21 and over) or just sit across from the stage and enjoy the live entertainment. The nightly entertainers here are usually very good. It's a nice atmosphere to hang out and relax with others in the early evening.

Raglan Road often has free live music in the bar, particularly on weekends – enjoy for the cost of a drink! (21 and over). There are also some lively outdoor seating areas outside of Raglan Road that may serve as a nice date location. The options for shopping, dining and entertainment are almost endless at Disney Springs. Whether you desire a quaint dining experience tucked away from the crowds or a lively environment loaded with energy, Disney Springs will likely have what you are looking for.

SIX

FREE FUN AT DISNEY'S BOARDWALK

Disney's Boardwalk is built around a lake and is beautifully themed to be reminiscent of Cape May or Coney Island in the 1940s.

It's fun just walking around and enjoying the atmosphere, especially in the evening! If you are staying on Disney property, you can use Disney transportation to get to the Boardwalk. If you have a car and are not visiting on the weekend you will usually be allowed to park at the Boardwalk for a few hours without charge.

The attendant at the parking gate will usually give you a FREE 3-hour parking permit so you can explore, shop and eat. While some of the restaurants are open at lunchtime, the best time to visit the Boardwalk is after sunset. It's beautifully lit up, romantic and magical.

READY. SET. DISNEY

Free at Disney's Boardwalk

Evenings on the Boardwalk are full of energy and excitement. Most evenings you will find entertaining street performers (jugglers, comedians, fire-eaters, jazz ensembles, etc.) We love to stroll on the Boardwalk in the evening, stopping for the shows along the way.

There are also many vendors selling inexpensive treats. You can try your luck at a carnival-style game (small cost) or sit and watch the Friendship Boats come and go on the lake. The Boardwalk bakery is a very popular spot to grab a pastry or dessert item.

You can also visit Jellyroll's (a dueling piano bar featuring sing-a-longs to your favorite pop tunes) for a $12 per person cover charge for guests 21 and over.

You might also want to check out <u>Atlantic Dance Hall</u>, which has dancing to DJ-spun Top 40 music most evenings with no cover charge. This hall is open to guests 21 years of age and over.

There is always something lively and fun to experience at the boardwalk. We recommend planning some time in your schedule to relax and enjoy this free Disney space.

READY. SET. DISNEY

SEVEN

DISNEY TRANSPORTATION FUN

Though Disney transportation serves the practical purpose of getting people where they need to go, it can also be an adventurous and Free way to explore the world of Disney.

Disney has an elaborate transportation system of boats, buses, monorails and more which can all be accessed for free from just about anywhere on Disney property. Boat rides are enjoyable any time, but they can be especially memorable and romantic at night.

Take the "inner" <u>Monorail</u> that circles the three Monorail resorts. From the Magic Kingdom, the route will take you through the Contemporary resort to the Magic Kingdom Ticket Center. From there you will continue on to the Polynesian resort, then the Grand Floridian resort and then back to the Magic Kingdom.

This is a great way to orient yourself and get a look at the Magic Kingdom resorts and an overview of the Magic Kingdom. You can get off and explore each resort, or just enjoy the ride and the view the beauty of Disney World. There is never a cost to ride the Monorail system.

<u>Cruise the loop around Crescent Lake</u>, which visits Epcot, Boardwalk, Yacht/Beach Club, Swan/Dolphin, and Disney's Hollywood Studios without going into the parks. There is

no cost to riding the boats and you can off and on at any of these locations – why not make a day of it?

<u>Seven Lagoons boat rides.</u> Take the boat that visits the Magic Kingdom, Contemporary, Wilderness Lodge and Ft. Wilderness or the boat that visits the Polynesian, Grand Floridian and Magic Kingdom (and you can get off at the Magic Kingdom and wander along the lake outside the gates. You can then continue your boat journey or hop on the monorail.

<u>Cruise from Port Orleans to Disney Springs and back</u>, along the Sassagoula River. This is another scenic boat ride, especially on a warm evening. There is no Cost for these boat rides, and it is a great way to see a good bit of Disney without a ton of effort. We love to take the boats as an alternative to the bus because it is more relaxing and usually less crowded.

<u>The New Disney Skyliner - Gondola System</u>

One of our favorite new adventures in Disney transportation is the Disney Skyliner. The hub for this new Gondola transportation experience is at the Caribbean

Beach Resort though you can access the Skyliner at The Rivera Resort, The Pop Century Resort or The Art of Animation Resort. You can also hop onto a Gondola at Epcot or Hollywood Studios. The Skyliner is very smooth, comfortable and enjoyable. In our opinion, the Skyliner is the most beautiful and relaxing way to transport from any of the Epcot resorts to Epcot or Hollywood Studios. The ride can also be a very romantic break for couples as well. We love it!

READY. SET. DISNEY

EIGHT

DISNEY'S TOWN OF CELEBRATION

Just a ten-minute drive from Disney World you can travel back in time to find the beautiful town of Celebration. This was originally a planned community developed by the Walt Disney Company. The town is a pedestrian-friendly, wonderful small town (think Mayberry!) It's easy to get to and full of quaint shops and relaxing adventure.

You can have a great time exploring the old-fashioned downtown area called Market Street. There are several memorable experiences you may want to pursue during your time at Disney.

Below are several ideas that you might consider during your visit to the town of Celebration. There are several things you can do for free and others that will cost you little. There are also a couple of splurges that you might enjoy as well.

READY. SET. DISNEY

<u>Explore the Lakeside Promenade</u> or the miles of walking paths and nature trails. This is a relaxing way to "get away" from the business of the parks and enjoy the outdoors. This may be a great way to spend an afternoon of evening if you are on park overload.

<u>Window shopping on Market Street</u>
The town of Celebration is loaded with wonderful specialty stores, numerous dining locations and quaint boutiques and Galleries. Market Street has scheduled monthly events, such as craft festivals, antique car shows, etc. You can contact the town of Celebration Chamber of Commerce to find the times and dates of these events.

<u>The Holiday Season at Celebration</u>
During the winter holidays, Market Street hosts an event called "Now Snowing Nightly."

During this wonderful season, it "snows" on Celebration's main street four times nightly and the town provides live entertainment and regular visits from Santa in his lakeside chalet, all for Free.

Visit the Bohemian Hotel Celebration
This beautiful hotel is located right downtown. Sit in one of the oversized wicker chairs, people-watch, and have a drink or coffee at the lobby bar.

Have an appetizer or dessert at one of the various local restaurants, including award-winning Spanish and Cuban cuisine!

Pick up some picnic items and head over to the Interactive Fountain to let the kids (or you) have a splash!

Kilwins Ice Cream
If you are in the mood for a sweet treat, why not treat yourself yourself to an ice-cream or lemonade from Kilwins Ice Cream and then enjoy it relaxing in one of the rocking chairs by the lake. It's a delicious way to spend an afternoon or evening.

READY. SET. DISNEY

NINE

DINING TIPS TO EAT WELL AND SAVE BIG!

Pass On The Meal Plan

Eating at Disney should be an adventure in itself. If you happen to be fortunate enough to receive the Disney meal plan for free with your package, great – enjoy it. However, Disney only offers the free meal plan on rare occasions, typically only sporadically during value seasons and when room and hopper tickets passes are included in your vacation package.

Otherwise, if you are on a rather tight budget, we recommend that you take a pass on the meal plan. We have found that there are many ways to eat well and have an awesome adventure at Disney while saving hundreds of dollars in the process. Granted, having the meal plan can be lots of fun but the high cost can be a bit much for anyone trying to save here and there.

We recommend that you plan your eating locations ahead of time. Making a plan on the spot when everyone is hungry and grumpy is not always the best way to foster an enjoyable dining experience. Make sure you plan around the busiest times of the day when waiting will be at a minimum.

Stock Your Room With Groceries

If you have the ability and space to bring some grocery items from home, it will pay to bring some along. Eating breakfast in your room to start the day or packing a lunch for the parks can add up to big savings throughout your stay.

If you have transportation and the ability to visit a local grocery store like Publix, you can stock up on snacks, drinks and lunch items. Make sure to request a room with a mini refrigerator when you book your room.

Another option for those who are unable to make it to the grocery store is to order your grocery items online through Amazon.com. Currently, when you order $35 or more in grocery items.
Amazon will deliver them to your room free of charge. This is a great way to save a little time and money while also conveniently stocking the refrigerator (or cooler).

Pack A Lunch And Snacks

If you can purchase groceries for your entire Disney vacation, packing a lunch for the park is a great way to save money. Many people are unaware that Disney allows coolers and food items to be brought into the park.

This is another reason to bring a stroller to the park even after your kids are old enough to walk on their own. Though you cannot bring glass bottles or alcoholic beverages into the park, you can bring back packs or coolers with everything you need for a fantastic lunch. There are several out of the way locations within each park to sit and enjoy a wonderful picnic without the hassle of waiting in long food lines.

You can cut your expenses even further if you have breakfast at your room before you leave for the parks.

Share Meals

If you would like to eat at a nicer restaurant without paying a ton more for food, you might consider eating at a non-buffet sit down restaurant and sharing meals. Many restaurants offer much larger meals that can be split between family members. The cost per meal will be more, but the overall expense is split in half if you share meals. Of course, you will want to include the cost of tipping when considering a sit-down meal.

Our favorite place to split meals is at Mama Melrose's on Grand Ave within Hollywood Studios. The meals at

READY. SET. DISNEY

Mama's are delicious with large portions and can easily be split between two people.

You will likely need to make reservations ahead to eat at Mama Melrose' but you will be glad that you did. Splitting the large pizzas at Via Napoli in Italy at Epcot is another great option.

We also love to split meals at "Be our Guest" in Belle's Castle at the Magic Kingdom. The adult meals are large enough to split and the atmosphere is magical. Getting reservations for lunch at Belle's can be tough so be sure to make reservations as early as possible. Dinner at Belle's Castle is a bit more expensive, and you can't split meals so target lunch time if you wanna save a little cash.

Another one of our favorite options for splitting meals is the Rainforest Café at the entrance to the Animal Kingdom. The nachos and burgers are huge, and the atmosphere is incredible for children and adults of all ages. There is also an amazing store to shop around in while you are waiting for your table. If you prefer dinosaurs to Gorillas, try T-Rex at Disney Springs. Both restaurants are owned by Landry's so if you have a Landry's card it will work at either location. Both restaurants are super fun for the whole family.

A Landry's Select Membership

If you have the time to visit Landry's Select Club online before your trip, you can sign up for a card that is good at all Landry's restaurants including the Rainforest Cafe.

The initial membership fee is $25 but you receive an immediate $25 meal credit on your new card for becoming a member which offsets the fee. You also receive a $25 reward for your birthday which is good the entire month of your birthday.

If you set your birthdate (probably not your actual birth date) to coincide with your trip, you will be able to use your $25 membership reward and your $25 birthday reward on your trip. Be sure to order your card a few weeks before your scheduled trip to allow time for the card to be delivered to your home.

If multiple members of your family or group have rewards and set their birthdates to coincide with the date of your trip, you save even more.

Plus, the card gets you expedited seating when you check in. This will be especially useful if you decide to eat at one of the Landry's restaurants at Disney Springs. Disney

READY. SET. DISNEY

Springs can have longer wait times because many people visit Disney Springs instead of visiting a Disney park since there is no admission fee to enter Disney Springs. We have used our Landry's card dozens of times over the years to save waiting time receive birthday rewards and to save money on items in the gift shop.

Look For The Fixings Stations

There are also counter service options that offer a large "fixings" station that greatly enhances the value of your meal. One of our favorites is Pecos Bill's at the Magic Kingdom. We order a side of the beans and rice and load them up at the fixings bar with cheese, sour cream and salsa.

Another great fixins station is located inside of Starlight Café'. There are several ingredients like cooked onions and cooked mushrooms to add to your burger, salad or sandwich in order to increase the deliciousness...

Share A Huge Snack

If you are craving a snack but want to save a little dough, there are many snack options that are so big you can split them and not feel cheated. Here are some of our favorites:

Some Huge Snacks At Magic Kingdom

The Waffle Bowl Sundae at The Plaza Ice Cream Parlor on Main Street is a family favorite. Wow! You might also try the huge Cookie Sundae at Storybook Treats in Fantasy Land or the gigantic Cinnamon Roll at Gaston's Tavern. Each of these treats are "largely" delicious and big enough to share with a friend.

Some Huge Snacks at Animal Kingdom

The Ice Cream Cookie at Dino Bites in Dino Land is almost impossible to eat without some assistance (Some of you are scoffing right now!!!) There is also a Colossal Cinnamon Roll at **Kusafari Coffee Shop and Bakery** in Africa. Yum and Yum!

Some Huge Snacks at Hollywood Studios

The huge cupcakes at Starring Rolls Café on Sunset Blvd – One of our all-time favorites is the Butterfinger cupcake. It's absolutely Delish. You might also like the Ice Cream Sandwiches and Bowls at Hollywood Scoops on Sunset Blvd. There are many delicious snacks at the Trolley Car on Hollywood Blvd as well and you can grab a Starbucks coffee there if you are a bit of a dunker.

We recently discovered that the Butterfinger cupcake is smaller than it used to be but it is still a very good cupcake. There are also many intriguing desserts at Starbucks close to the park entrance along with the Butterfinger cupcake.

Some Huge Snacks at Epcot

Wow! Epcot snacks...where to begin? The larger pastries at Les Halles Boulangerie – Patisserie in France are super amazing. We love the elephant ear pastries and the eclairs. For a good variety, many of the snacks at the Sunshine Seasons Eatery in the Land are really good.

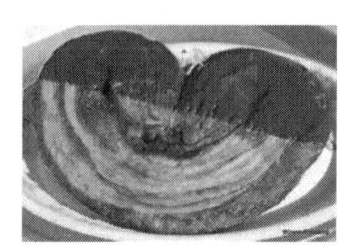

We also love the desserts at Kringla Bakery in Norway. The School Bread, Crème Horns and a variety of pretzels are some of our family favorites. Germany has some great desserts you might want to check out as well. Try the caramel or chocolate covered apple, a caramel salted cup cake or a bag of caramel popcorn. Yowza.

If you happen to be visiting Disney during one of the annual festivals put on at Epcot. (Wine and food, Flower and Garden etc.) A whole new world of snacks and comfort food will be open to you. Pace yourself and enjoy...

Kids Meals

Many of the kid's meals at Disney World are actually a great value compared to the cost and quantity of food in some adult meals.

Though they are listed for children under 9, we have been told many times that adults may order from the kid's menu if they like - So, we have done so on many occasions.

Each kids' meal comes with a drink, and two snacks. Purchasing a kid's meal at a location that also offers the fixings bar will maximize your value.

It is often a better value to purchase 2 kids meals for each adult rather than one adult meal. This way drinks and snacks are included with your meal and the food quantity is greater. More food for less money = greater value – It just makes sense.

Order Out Pizza

There are several pizza places bordering Disney property that will deliver directly to your room or resort lobby. If you can wait to eat until you get back to your room, this can be a great money saving idea. Our favorite places to order pizza from are Giordano's (Chicago Deep Dish style) and Flappers. We have also had pizza delivered to resort lobbies and pools on occasion.

READY. SET. DISNEY

Best Value Restaurants At Disney

<u>The Magic Kingdom</u> – We love Pecos Bills in Frontier Land because of the fixings bar and Cosmic Ray's Starlight Café in Tomorrow Land for the variety of options.

Another good option is Pinocchio Haus in Frontier Land. We love the fresh bread sticks and marinara sauce. If you want a savory snack, this is a good option at a fair price. We also enjoy the savory and sweet snacks at Gaston's and of course some people can't leave Magic Kingdom without having a turkey leg from one of the side carts in Frontier Land – To each his own, I suppose.

<u>The Animal Kingdom</u> – The Satu'li Canteen in Avatar Land has a super great atmosphere and a variety of wonderful food options. There are also free refills on beverages of which we take full advantage. Pizzafari has good pizza and lots of seating both inside and outside. Also, we love the flatbreads, Gyro sandwiches and the kids rib meals at the Harambe Market in Africa. The Yak and Yeti counter service has very good curry.

Hollywood Studios There are a great variety of options at ABC Commissary on Commissary Lane. Our favorite counter service pizza at Disney World is PizzeRizzo on Grand Blvd. They have free refills on beverages and really good pizza. Again, splitting meals at Mama Melrose is our favorite meal sharing option at Disney.

Epcot – Wow, there are so many great places to eat at Epcot. However, for value we recommend Sunshine Seasons at The Land. They have tons of options for meals and desserts. Drink refills are free here as well. The kids Salmon meal is delicious and inexpensive. The ham and cheese croissants at the bakery in France are delish and very reasonably priced.

The sandwiches at Kringla Bakery in Norway are super good and reasonably priced. I especially enjoy the club sandwich, it's large enough to split or it will fill you up if you are especially hungry. There are counter service options within each country that you can choose from if you are looking for a certain kind of food. Your choice will depend a lot on the kinds of food you most enjoy. I'll bet you will find something you like.

READY. SET. DISNEY

SECTION TWO

Preparing For Your Disney Vacation

READY. SET. DISNEY

TEN

When To Go? Where To Stay?

Download My Disney Experience App

One of the first things you will want to do in preparing for your Disney trip will be to download the My Disney Experience app on your phone.

The <u>My Disney Experience App</u> is extremely helpful to your overall Disney vacation. The app allows you to make reservations, reserve your Fast Passes, check on ride wait times, look at restaurant menus and more.

You can do these things without the app, but it's much more convenient using the app. <u>The Guide Maps</u> that we have prepared for you will work best as a compliment to the My Disney Experience app.

Another app that you may want to consider downloading to your phone, especially if you have children, is the "Play at Disney Parks" app. This app is loaded with games that can be enjoyed by the entire family while making your way through each park and while waiting in lines. This app will also be necessary for some of the interactive adventures available within the parks.

READY. SET. DISNEY

We recommend that you download these apps well before your trip. This will allow you to explore the parks a bit, check out current ride wait times and plan out your route through each park.

Planning Your Disney Trip Date

Though you may not have a good deal of flexibility in your schedule, planning when to take your trip to Disney World is much more important than many realize.

Prices vary by season so choosing to go to Disney during a low season is a good way to reduce expenses.

Also, the parks are much less crowded during low seasons which results in shorter lines and an overall more enjoyable Disney experience.

Though crowds are inevitable at Disney, there are certain times when the crowds are smaller. So, unless you have no other option, we strongly recommend that you choose to visit Disney during a low traffic season if possible.

When Are The Low And High Seasons?

Reminding you of the chart from chapter two (we have re-inserted it below), historically, the least busy days at Disney World are in the winter and Fall.

Notice that there are peaks during the holidays and spring break. Once again, we will remind you of the following information...

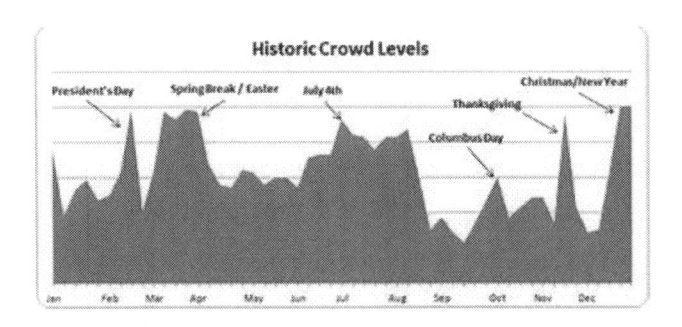

Historic Crowd Levels

(Labeled peaks: President's Day, Spring Break / Easter, July 4th, Columbus Day, Thanksgiving, Christmas/New Year)

Overall, the month of September, late November and early December are the least busy seasons followed by January, early February and early November. We have found that late February and early March to be fairly tolerable as well.

This pattern is generally consistent from year to year though it is important that you are aware of special events (i.e. marathons, Halloween parties, specialty days etc.) Special events will typically cause the parks to swell even during low seasons.

Note also that weekends are generally much busier than weekdays. Fridays through the day are typically less busy than Friday evenings. Friday evenings and Saturdays are usually the busiest times of the week to visit the parks and Sundays, though less congested than Saturdays can still be a bit of a hassle.

Once again, if your trip to Disney World will feature days of relaxation with a little less time within the parks on certain days, we recommend that you choose the weekends to relax and explore rather than the less busy weekdays. Being at the parks at the least busy times will increase your enjoyment level.

Is There A Best Day For Each Park?

You may be wondering if there is a pattern to the busyness of each park; Is a certain park better on one day than another? Should we plan our week according to these patterns?

The answer is yes, but it's not always the same day throughout every season and extremely busy seasons are typically packed every day of the week. So just be aware, if you are visiting Disney during one of the busy seasons, it's going to be busy everywhere.

Using the tips in this guide will help alleviate some of your stress. However, crowds are crowds. Take heart, there is still magic amid the madness.

<u>In general</u>, there's a pattern to the busyness of each park. These will not always hold true but should remain fairly consistent apart from special event days or holidays. In general, the pattern listed below is a good rule to follow.

We use the following guidelines to help us decide which park to visit on which day. However, sometimes we go ahead and visit the park that we prefer to visit on a given day without regard to how busy the park may be.

The Best Days To Attend Each Park

Monday – Hollywood Studios

Tuesday – Magic Kingdom (Avoid Friday nights and Saturdays if possible)

Wednesday – Epcot (Always busier after 5 pm)

Thursday – Animal Kingdom

Friday – Animal Kingdom

Saturday & Sunday – Busy Everywhere. Go with your heart…

Again, these are not hard and fast rules. There are many factors that can contribute to park attendance on any given day. In general, we stay away from a park that is holding a special event, that is offering extra magic hours for that day or that doesn't fit in the chart above.

Florida Resident Annual Passholders

Remember that Florida residents with Annual Passes tend to visit more on the weekends and evenings so Friday night through Sunday afternoon can be very busy times. This does not hold true during holiday seasons when everyone is off work and/or on a school break.

READY. SET. DISNEY

Top Secret Park Tip

Pay attention to special events such as marathons or seasonal celebrations. These events typically cause the parks to swell – avoid these special occasions if you want to escape the crowds.

Some events such as "Mickey's Not So Scary Halloween Party" will affect the Magic Kingdom only. Disney Marathons or special visit days will affect each park.

Typically, all the parks will be busier on the days before, during and after these special events.

What About Weather?

Ironically, some of the least busy times at Disney World are also some of the best weather days of the year in Orlando. Apart from the risk of an errant hurricane in the fall, the weather is cooler, less humid and, overall, more pleasant than spring break and the busy summer months.

This is yet another reason to choose a low season if you can work it out.

Where Should We Stay?

We are often asked if it is better to stay on Disney property or just outside of Disney at a non-Disney resort or hotel. Our answer is usually "both" or "it depends," which doesn't sound like a helpful answer at all – haha.

I suppose the correct answer depends on the goals of your vacation and the budget you are working with. Though Disney is a magical place with wonderful resort accommodations, staying off Disney property can make sense depending on the circumstances.

Advantages To Staying Off Disney Property

Staying at a resort or hotel just outside of Disney property can be a good option for several reasons.

1) First, there are many beautiful and luxurious <u>resorts very close to Disney</u> that offer promotional or discounted rates if you are traveling during a low season

2) In addition, if you are willing to sit through a "90 minute" resort tour and presentation you can <u>stay for even less</u> and often receive a couple free day passes to a Disney park. Though these timeshare tours can be high pressure - did I hear someone say "understatement"? you usually receive free breakfast or lunch in addition to the promotional offer.

3) If you are traveling with a larger family or extended family, Disney has very few reasonably priced options. Many resorts close to Disney offer 2, 3 or 4-bedroom <u>condos that will accommodate much larger families.</u>

4) There are also a great number of <u>larger homes</u> for rent in the Orlando area available on sites like VRBO or Air B 'n' B that can accommodate larger families or groups. Though these options may lack a bit of the magic of a Disney resort, they may be a better fit for your circumstances.

READY. SET. DISNEY

5) Also, staying off Disney property opens up the opportunity to save some money by choosing to eat some or all of your <u>meals at restaurants outside of Disney</u>.

You may still choose to have some very memorable meals on Disney property, but you would have the flexibility to choose from the many options outside of Disney as well.

6) Though we greatly enjoy the magic of Disney, there are actually <u>many things to do in Orlando</u> apart from going to Disney World. True, Disney is the happiest place on Earth. However, you may want to spend some time exploring one of the many <u>other options in Orlando</u> and the surrounding areas. Universal Studios, Sea World, The Kennedy Space Center, one of the many great beaches, etc.

You may be asking: "<u>but what if I don't have transportation?</u>" Yes, that's the biggest catch to staying off Disney property. So, unless you drive to Disney, if you plan to stay off Disney property, it may be a good idea to rent a car. Shuttle transportation can often be unreliable and restrictive, it may pay off to have the freedom and flexibility of your own transportation.

Advantages To Staying On Disney Property

From our perspective, staying on Disney property has several advantages. Here are a few to consider:

1) When you stay on Disney property, you are permitted to <u>reserve your Fast Passes much earlier</u> – 60 days in advance of your arrival date. This can be fairly significant when considering the difficulty of getting Fast Passes for some of the most popular rides at each park.

2) Resort guests are also permitted to enter certain parks early and / or stay late – this is called Extra Magic Hours.

3) There is transportation to anywhere within Disney property right from the entrance of each Disney resort. If you don't like the idea of figuring out how to get from one place to another, don't stress, let Disney do it for you.

4) Staying on Disney property allows you and your loved ones to experience the Disney magic 24 / 7. There is something special about staying on Disney property. If your budget allows for it, go ahead and book it.

Uber and Other Catch A Ride Companies

Though Disney transportation will not take you off Disney property, there are several options to consider if you would like to visit a restaurant or location off Disney property.

From our experience, you may consider using an Uber or another catch a ride company instead of a taxi. Uber is cheaper and usually quicker. However, Uber is not permitted to pick you up at the Orlando airport. We suggest that you download the Uber app before you leave so you are prepared to use it when you need it.

Our Favorite Disney Resorts

Over the years we have had the opportunity to stay or extensively visit nearly every Disney resort or hotel. Below we list our top picks for each resort category.

READY. SET. DISNEY

Though each Disney resort is special in its own way, the choices we offer have been clear favorites for our family over the years. Hopefully our recommendations will help you as you plan accommodations for your trip.

Our Favorite Resorts In Each Category

Deluxe	Moderate	Value
Polynesian	Caribbean Beach	Art of Animation
Animal Kingdom	Port Orleans	Pop Century
Wilderness Lodge	Coronado Springs	All Star Resorts
Grand Floridian		

Of course, if there were no consideration whatsoever for cost, The Grand Floridian may get a little more love on our list of deluxe resorts. However, cost makes the Grand Floridian somewhat impractical for many guests.

All deluxe resorts can be expensive, but the Grand Floridian is usually in a category of its own when it comes to pricing. The resort choice that you make will be based on several factors including: the size of your party, your style preference and your vacation budget.

Staying at a deluxe resort is typically a large price jump from staying at a moderate resort. This is also true when jumping from a value resort to a moderate resort.

In our opinion, when choosing a value resort, Disney's Art of Animation resort is miles ahead of the other value resorts. Similarly, when choosing a moderate resort, Disney's Caribbean Beach Resort is miles ahead of the other moderates.

This may be why these two resorts are typically booked before the other resorts in their category. If you want to stay at one of these resorts, try booking at least 6 months out.

Of course, these are only our opinions based on a personal comparison of resort atmosphere, pool area, food courts and rooms. Each Disney resort is unique and will appeal to different people for different reasons.

There are only certain Disney resorts that offer rooms large enough for families of 6. They are Disney's Art of Animation Resort, Disney's All-Star Music Resort and most deluxe resorts.

Port Orleans Riverside and The Caribbean Beach Resort offer rooms that will sleep 4 adults and many rooms offer an additional child size trundle bed.

Disney Vacation Club

The Disney Vacation Club is Disney's version of timeshare vacation ownership. Renting a week from an DVC owner can be a more reasonable way to stay at a super nice Disney Resort. If this interests you, we have written a bit more about it in chapter two.

Top Secret Tip On Room & Ticket Up-Grades

Disney is known for upgrades. It will often payoff to ask for an upgrade whenever you speak to a Disney representative. Over the years we have been upgraded to a higher tiered room on several occasions.

READY. SET. DISNEY

Also, we have heard stories of people being upgraded from a moderate resort to a deluxe resort or from one park per day tickets to tickets with hopper passes etc. If you are traveling in a low season, your chances of receiving an upgrade are pretty good. So, whether you are speaking with a Disney Rep before you leave, at check-in or at a theme park, it doesn't hurt to ask.

<u>Online check-in</u> may be faster, but a major disadvantage is that you miss an opportunity to ask for an upgrade.

ELEVEN

Making Your Dining Reservations

Magical Meal Experiences

Choosing the right restaurants for your family or group is a big part of the overall Disney experience. Knowing when and where to eat that perfect meal will help contribute a great deal to the Magic of each day. Waiting until you arrive to make your dining choices may limit your options and increase your stress level.

We have already given you some of our top discount dining tips in Chapter 9. Later, we give you our favorite Disney restaurants with our comments and evaluation in the Dining Section in Chapter 15.

We will even give you a list of our top 10 favorite dining locations at Disney World in Chapter 16. We hope our dining suggestions will help make your Disney vacation a bit more magical and much more delicious.

Cinderella's Royal Table

It is difficult, when considering the dining options at Disney, to avoid a discussion of the Cinderella Castle. Yes, it is pricey. Yes, it requires two table service allotments on the meal plan. And, yes… you should do it anyway if you can afford it.

In order to save a little toward your meal in the Castle, why not pack sandwiches and make this the only "sitdown" meal of the day? This might help lighten the blow a bit.

Eating at the Cinderella Castle is a magical adventure that everyone should experience at least once. The food is very good, you get to meet Cinderella and Prince Charming and each person is treated like a prince or princess for a couple incredible hours. Be careful though, it kinda went to my head when the waiter kept calling me "my lord…"

There is also a photo shoot included with your meal where you will receive a photo to remember your magical day with Cinderella and Prince Charming. If you want to eat in the Cinderella Castle, you will want to make reservations 180 days before your check in date.

Seriously, do not wait until 179 days before you leave. You will need to call or book online first thing in the morning 180 before your trip. If you are inside of 180 days already, don't freak out, keep trying - there are cancellations from time to time.

If you are already at Disney with no reservation you can show up at the Castle and ask if there have been any cancellations. Often (but not always) you can get seated the same day. This approach also works very well at Belle's Castle for lunch.

You should make your dining reservations by order of difficulty rather than making them chronologically. In other words, make the reservations that are most difficult to secure first. We list the most difficult reservations in the restaurant section in chapter 15.

Top Secret Reservation Tip #1

If you can't quite decide on the best time to make a dining reservation go ahead and reserve two different time slots. Once the date is closer just cancel the reservation you don't want and keep the one that best fits your schedule.

Be sure to cancel all unwanted reservations by midnight the day before the reservation so your credit card won't be charged.

Also, book your most difficult reservations closer to the end of your stay. You can book all your reservations 180 days from the start of your vacation. This means that if you will be staying at Disney for a week, you can book your final day of reservations 187 days in advance.

Booking online will give you a one-hour head-start over booking over the phone since online booking begins at 6 am eastern time and phone reservations begin at 7 am.

Top Secret Reservation Tip #2

We usually find it a bit much to schedule breakfast, lunch and dinner at a Disney dining location while also making room for the occasional snack.

We usually purchase some fruit, trail mix, granola bars, cereal etc. to eat in our room each morning then we have

READY. SET. DISNEY

an early lunch and semi-late dinner. This seems to work great for us.

You may also choose to have a hearty breakfast and a lighter lunch. We love to pack PB and J sandwiches for lunch. This way we can eat them on the go or while we wait in one of the lines.

The Basic meal plan coincides with this eating strategy by giving you 1 counter service, 1 sit down and 2 snacks per day. We find this to be more than adequate...and we LOVE to eat.

TWELVE

Some Advice On Disney Meal Plans

Should We Purchase The Meal Plan?

Many first-time visitors to Disney ask if they should purchase the meal plan or just pay for meals "on the fly." In general, you can only save money by purchasing the meal plan if you intend to eat most or all your meals on Disney property at Disney Buffets or at some of the more expensive Disney restaurants.

The meal plan can add a considerable amount to the overall expense of your vacation, but it might also allow you to eat at some restaurants that you would likely not pay to eat at otherwise.

The real value of the meal plan is in the convenience not the savings. Also, when you are on the meal plan, you feel a little less guilty about ordering whatever you want at the most expensive restaurants since you have already paid for it by purchasing the meal plan. As a dad, I enjoy being able to say "just order whatever you want" for a change.

Typically, you are not permitted to add a meal plan to your stay unless you add it to a package. The meal plan is based on the number of days you will be staying at a Disney resort. There is also a minimum ticket purchase required as well.

So, if you are staying off Disney property or purchase your tickets and room separately to take advantage of room only discounts, you will not be permitted to add a meal plan to your tickets. Each meal plan includes a refillable mug that can be used at any resort but not at the parks.

Below we outline the pros and cons of each meal plan type. We understand that one choice does not fit all. Your meal plan choice will be determined by your budget, your appetite and the kinds of restaurants you want to visit while at Disney. Hopefully, we can help you in making the right choice for your family or group.

The Deluxe Meal Plan *(3 sit-down meals, 2 snacks per day + 1 refillable mug)*

We have found that if you purchase the deluxe meal plan it's almost impossible to eat all the food. Three sit-down meals per day and 2 snacks is a lot for any one person – especially when you consider that many of the sit-down meals are all you can eat buffets.

Plus, taking the time out of your schedule for 3 sit-down meals each day will take a big chunk of time from your daily schedule and may hinder you from some other things you may want to do.

Unless you want long frequent breaks in your day and plan to eat a ton of food, the deluxe meal plan might be a bit too much.

You can substitute a counter service for a sit-down meal if you prefer, but you lose the true value of the deluxe meal plan since sit-down meals are far more expensive than counter service meals.

The deluxe meal plan would be a good idea for those who want to experience a few of the more expensive dining options that require 2 sit-down meal tickets like... Cinderella Castle, the California Grill, LeCelier, or The Spirit of Aloha.

The Basic Meal Plan *(1 sit-down, 1 counter service and 2 snacks per day + 1 refillable mug)*

The Basic Meal Plan is a good option for most families. Believe it or not, it is still very difficult to eat all the food. We have found that using our sit-down meals at buffets or character meals is the best value.

Don't waste your sit-down meals on restaurants where you could eat relatively inexpensively without having the meal plan.

The Quick Service Meal Plan *(2 counter service and 2 snacks per day + 1 refillable mug)*

The Quick Service Meal Plan will save you a little money if you are planning on eating most of your meals on Disney property but don't want to spend a bunch on sit-down meals. It won't save you a ton of money, but there are several advantages to getting it.

READY. SET. DISNEY

First, it's really convenient for everyone in the family to be able to pay for their meal by using their magic bands. This is especially true if everyone is grabbing their meal from a different location.

Also, kids love the freedom and POWER they experience by being able to pay for themselves by scanning their own magic band.

When it comes to counter service options at Disney, there are actually a zillion to choose from. Ok, maybe a few less than that, but there are still a ton. So, the quick service meal plan gives you a wide variety of options.

Mobile Ordering

One cool feature that Disney added last year at each of the Disney parks is mobile ordering. Its quick and easy through the My Disney Experience app. Let's say you're waiting in line for a ride, but you want to eat as soon as you get off. Just click on the app, find the restaurant you want, place your order and go straight to the front of the line to pick up your food when you get off the ride. Its sweet.

No Meal Plan

One of the advantages of taking our family to Disney multiple times per year for over two decades is that we have discovered many money-saving alternatives to purchasing one of the meal plans. If you skipped over the discount dining information earlier in this book, you may want to check it out. This information may be helpful if you are trying to do Disney for less. We have found that you can still eat like princes and princesses without paying a royal price for each meal.

Also, if you choose to bypass a Disney meal plan, the Restaurant section later in this book may be helpful information to look over before making any dining reservations. Choosing the right dining experience is a huge part of making the most of your Disney vacation. Take some time to plan out your meal options and make reservations before you arrive.

Top Secret Dining Tip #1

On occasion, Disney will offer the Free Dining Plan for a limited time along with a resort / ticket package. This deal is most frequently offered in the Fall, but it has occasionally been offered at other times throughout the year. Also, we have found that the free meal plan is rarely publicized, and the offers are typically gone within a week of the release date.

If you can travel during one of these special offer periods and plan to stay at a Disney resort, adding the free meal plan is a no brainer if you can get it.

Top Secret Dining Tip #2

Using a snack credit at Starbucks can be a great value for coffee lovers. Adding expresso shots or syrups to your order is included for no extra charge. This means that you could potentially get an $8-$9 value out of one snack credit. We list some of our favorite snack options for each park later in the restaurant section.

Top Secret Dining Tip #3

Most every counter service and snack location at each park will give you cups of ice or ice water for free. This may be a better option than carrying around a water bottle that you need to keep refilling at the drinking fountain. Plus, it's colder and more refreshing. If you have a water bottle with you at the park, you could always pour the ice water into your own bottle if you prefer.

THIRTEEN

Reserving Your Fast Passes

When Can I Reserve My Fast Passes?

The first day you will be permitted to reserve your Fast Passes is 60 days before your arrival date - if you are staying on Disney property; you can reserve your Fast Passes through the <u>My Disney experience app</u>.

FP Choices

Your FP choices will depend on whether you plan to arrive at your park of choice early in the morning or sometime later in the day. If you plan to arrive when the park opens, you have the option to go to some of the rides that will have longer wait times later in the day.

Regardless of your arrival time, it will pay off to reserve your Fast Passes for the most popular attractions a little later in the day when wait times usually go up.

This strategy will be especially important if you are traveling to Disney during one of the busy seasons mentioned earlier in this book.

READY. SET. DISNEY

Which Fast Passes Do I Reserve?

The Fast Passes that you choose will depend on the age of your children and / or your personal attraction preferences. In the outline below, we give you our general thoughts on FP choices.

In the **Daily Guide Maps**, later in this book, we give specific age-appropriate FP recommendations for families. In fact, the Daily Guide Maps are designed to make your journey through each Disney park flow effortlessly.

Fast Pass Options By Park – Our recommendation for each age category is underlined.

Magic Kingdom FP Options

All Ages - The Jungle Cruise, <u>The Pirates of the Caribbean</u>, Buzz Lightyear Ranger Spin

Older kids and adults – Splash Mountain (A top choice especially on hot days), <u>Space Mountain</u>, Thunder Mountain Railroad

Younger kid & ups - <u>The Seven Dwarves Mine Train</u>, Under the Sea with Ariel - The Little Mermaid, Peter Pan's Flight.

Toddlers & up – <u>The Barnstormer</u>, Dumbo the Flying Elephant, Winnie The Pooh, Character Greetings

Animal Kingdom FP Options

All Ages - Na'Vi River Journey, The Kilimanjaro Safari, It's Tough To Be A Bug

Older kids and adults – Expedition Everest, Kali River Rapids, Dinosaur

Younger kids & up – Avatar Flight of Passage

Toddlers & up – Tricera Top Spin, Character Greetings

Hollywood Studios FP Options

All Ages – Frozen Sing Along, Beauty and the Beast Live on Stage, Fantasmic

Older kids and adults – Rock n Roller Coaster, Twilight Zone Tower of Terror

Younger kids & up – Toy Story Mania, Slinky Dog Dash, Millennium Falcon – Smugglers Run. Currently, the Rise of the Resistance experience is not available as a FP; in order to participate you must arrive early to the park and register for a group experience later in the day.

Toddlers & up – Alien Swirling Saucers, Disney Junior Live on Stage, Disney Junior Dance Party, Muppet 3D, Character Greetings

READY. SET. DISNEY

Epcot FP Options

All Ages – <u>Spaceship Earth</u>, Living with the Land, The Seas with Nemo and Friends

Older kids and adults – <u>Test Track</u>

Younger kids & up – <u>Soarin</u>, <u>Frozen Ever After</u>, Mission Space

Toddlers & up – Turtle Talk with Crush, Character Greetings

Child Swap

Don't forget to ask for a child swap ticket on rides where your youngest kids are too small to ride. One adult can ride with the older kids and then the other adult can use the child swap ticket to ride with the kids.

This allows both adults to ride while only one waits in line. This also provides the adult who stays with the younger children some time to grab a snack and spend some quality time with the kids who aren't big enough to ride. Everyone wins!

Top Secret FP Tip #1

Everyone assumes that each person receives only 3 Fast Passes per day, period. We have found that this is not necessarily true. After you have used all your Fast Passes, find one of the kiosks located inside the park and scan your magic band.

Often, especially when the park is less busy, you will receive another Fast Pass. We have discovered that you may be able to do this repeatedly throughout the day especially if your Fast Passes are earlier in the day. Epcot and Hollywood Studios use a tiered Fast Pass system, meaning you may choose only one option from tier one and then two options from tier 2.

Currently, tier one attractions at Epcot are Soarin, Test Track and Frozen Ever After. Tier one options at Hollywood Studios are Tower of Terror, Rockin Roller Coaster, Slinky Dog Dash and Toy Story Mania.

Top Secret FP Tip #2

If you don't mind splitting up your group, you can reduce your wait times significantly by waiting in a single rider line. The rides at Disney that offer a single rider line are Test Track, Expedition Everest and Rockin' Roller Coaster.

Also, if you want the best ride experience, ask if you can ride in the front on Expedition Everest and Rockin' Roller Coaster and in the back on Thunder Mountain Railroad. This may add a few minutes to your wait time, but it's worth the wait.

READY. SET. DISNEY

FOURTEEN

Disney Dining Guide

In the Restaurant Section we decided not to bog you down with a list of every possible dining and snack location inside Disney World. You can access an exhaustive list of dining locations and menus on the My Disney Experience app or through the Disney website. Our goal is just to tell you what we love and what we don't and let you decide from there.

Over the years, we have had the unique opportunity of eating at nearly every restaurant within Disney property, many of them multiple times. This gives us the unique opportunity to help you save time and not waste your money on mediocre dining experiences.

We have also been able to watch our kid's meal choices change as they have grown older. We hope that our suggestions will help you make dining choices that best fit your family or group. Also, we love atmosphere so many of our preferences are based as much on as atmosphere as they are on value. Just an FYI...

What we would like to give you in this section is inside information and evaluation of some of our favorite restaurants and snack locations throughout Disney World.

Also, we would like to offer some solid advice for those who would like to eat well but pay less. Here are our suggestions for each park. If you are looking for budget dining options, check out our dining suggestions earlier in this book (Chapter 9)

Magic Kingdom Dining Options

Counter Service Options

In our view, the best Counter Service Options at the Magic Kingdom are <u>Be Our Guest</u> in Fantasy Land, <u>Pecos Bill's</u> in Frontier Land and <u>Cosmic Ray's Starlight Café</u> in Tomorrow Land.

We love <u>Be Our Guest</u> because it is, in our opinion, the most magical counter service option in Disney World. Though it is a somewhat pricier counter service option, the food is tasty, and the atmosphere is magical.

We love to sit in the Ball or Rose room, but each room is beautiful and magical. As a bonus, there are free self-serve refills on drinks. Though Be Our Guest is a counter service option for lunch, you will still need a reservation to eat here.

Our kids love the Croque Monsieur and Mrs. Potts Turkey Sandwich. The cupcakes are super good. Stay away from the lemon puff, it's dreadful (again, just our opinion).

<u>Pecos Bill's</u> is a great option for older kids with a large appetite. You can order a burger and load it with toppings from the toppings bar (including cooked mushrooms).

Also, you can change one of your sides to rice and beans and cover them with sour cream, cheese and salsa from the toppings bar; it's a meal in itself.

The Fajita Platter is large as well, and you load it up even more by visiting the fixins bar.

Cosmic Ray's Starlight Café has the greatest variety for picky eaters as well as a sweet fixins bar. There is a large dining area with music played by Cosmic Ray himself. The atmosphere is fun and exciting for both the kid and the kid at heart. Your gonna love Cosmic Ray.

Pinocchio Village Haus – We love the Pizza Flatbreads and breadsticks

Columbia Harbor House – Many great Sea food choices. My wife loves the Lobster Roll.

Sit-Down Options (1 table service allowance)

Ohana (At the Polynesian Resort) – This is one of our very favorite sit-down dining options at Disney. The atmosphere is tropical with an Island feel. The food is endless and fantastic. There is singing and Hawaiian group participation games for the kids as well.

This restaurant can be both a romantic experience for couples and a fun time for kids. In our opinion, it's hard to beat dinner at Ohana.

Request a seat by the window, you might get lucky and get a view of the fireworks. No reservation? Don't panic, reservations often open up the day before so keep checking for availability on The My Disney Experience App.

READY. SET. DISNEY

If you are unable to make a reservation, you can just show up at the Polynesian resort and put your name in. They can often fit you in if you are willing to wait for a bit.

Be Our Guest – Though you can have a similar dining experience at Belle's Castle for less at lunch time, it gets even more magical for dinner. Dinner portions are larger with a variety of menu options. You will be greeted by an entire cast of Beauty and the Beast characters while dining in one of three enchanted rooms. You will want to book this one 180 days before your check in date if possible.

Park Fare (At the Grand Floridian Resort) – This is our choice for the best princess character dining close to the Magic Kingdom. The food is good with tons of variety on the buffet. Don't be in a huge hurry, it may take the princesses a while to make it to your table.

Crystal Palace – This is our choice for the best character dining without leaving the Magic Kingdom. The food buffet is good. Maybe not quite as fancy as Park Fare, but a wonderful experience, nonetheless. Reserve the first lunch or dinner spot available for quicker seating and character greeting opportunities.

Tony's Town Square Restaurant – This may be the best sit-down non-character dining experience at Magic Kingdom. A full menu of Italian fare and a nice relaxing atmosphere.

Jungle Navigation Co. – I would avoid this place. Not good. And we can't say that about many places at Disney. Maybe they were having a bad day, but we aren't willing to take any more chances to find out.

Premium Options (2 table service allowances)

Cinderella's Royal Table – Most Magical experience at Disney. Expensive, but everyone should do it once if possible. You might consider going for a late lunch rather than an early dinner to save $. There are many of the same meal options for a lower cost if you don't have the meal plan. The last available lunch time is 2:30 – 3 pm. Book 180 days before check in date.

Spirit of Aloha (At the Polynesian Resort) – Great show and good food, but dollar for dollar we would choose Ohana. The food is similar at both restaurants. You basically pay an additional meal allowance or a much higher price to see the show. That being said, it's a wonderful outdoor experience with a unique Polynesian feel. This may be an adventure that you want to experience with your family at least once.

California Grill (At the Contemporary Resort) – Very good food and great view of the fireworks. We are not as fond of the "atmosphere" of the Contemporary when compared with some of the other deluxe resorts. Personal preference I suppose.

Plus, eating here will cost you two table service allowances. Again, choose Ohana for 1 table service allowance instead unless you just have your lil ole heart set on it.

READY. SET. DISNEY

Magic Kingdom Snack Options

<u>Gaston's</u> in Fantasy Land – The Cinnamon Roll is hugamongous (you could easily split it). They also have cup cake's and Lefou's Brew – a tasty punch that is a good alternative to soda.

<u>Main Street Bakery</u> (Starbucks) – Tons of great snack options and of course...Starbucks coffee

<u>Storybook Treats in Fantasy Land</u> – Probably the best Sundae at any park. Huge and yummy.

<u>Plaza Ice Cream Parlor on Main St</u> – Great Waffle Bowl Sundaes. Also, big enough to split.

<u>Pecos Bills</u> – My girls love to stop here for a jalapeno pretzel from time to time

<u>Popcorn Stands</u> – If your family likes popcorn, consider purchasing the refillable popcorn bucket for $10. It's refillable for your entire stay for $1.50 at any park. It pays for itself with a couple refills and it's a nice souvenir. If you return to Disney, bring your refillable bucket. They will refill it even though you purchased it on a prior visit.

Animal Kingdom Dining Options

Counter Service Options

From our perspective, the best Counter Service Options at the Animal Kingdom are <u>Satu'li Canteen</u> at Pandora – The World of Avatar, <u>Harambe' Market</u> in Africa and <u>Pizzafari</u> on Discovery Island.

The Satu'li Canteen has a variety of options for adults and children. The wood-fired beef and chicken entrée options are very tasty. Our kids love the hamburger pods and the free drink refills.

One huge benefit of dining at Satu'li is the atmosphere of Pandora. Regardless of your dining plans, make sure to visit this area of the Animal Kingdom after dark – its Magical.

Harambe' Market is a great option for couples or families with older children. The rib dinners are very good, and the flatbread sandwiches are large and delicious as well.

Pizzafari has a large dining area and some great pizza and breadsticks. If you aren't up for pizza, try a shrimp or chicken salad. This a good option for little ones because you can eat inside or outside and typically kids love pizza.

Yak and Yeti Local Foods Café – We love the Teriyaki beef bowls and egg rolls.

Restaurantosaurus – Good burgers and dogs but you can also choose a sandwich or salad.

Sit-Down Options (1 table service allowance)

The Rainforest Café - (At the entrance to the Animal Kingdom) – This is also one of our very favorite sit-down dining options at Disney. If you have kids, the atmosphere at the Rainforest Café is difficult to top.

The food choices are extensive and fabulous. We love the huge burgers, the awesome appetizer, and the chicken sandwiches. If you want to splurge, go for the steak and mojo bones (ribs).

This restaurant can be a ton of fun for couples or families. Over the years, we have played "I spy" with our girls during our dining experience - there are loads of tropical animals, butterflies, birds and plants to add complexity to the game.

Every 20 minutes or so there is a tropical storm that causes the animals to "go wild." It truly is "a wild place to eat and shop"

In our opinion, dinner at The Rainforest Café is a must if you have never dined here. Also, if you are not on the meal plan, you can eat here cheaper than at one of the Disney buffets. Request a seat by the waterfall or large fish tank if there is one available.

Dining at the Rainforest will not require a reservation unless you plan to eat at the Rainforest in Disney Springs. Don't, the one at the Animal Kingdom is nicer and far less busy. We have given additional tips in the "Dining Tips To Eat Well And Save Big" section in chapter 9" that may help you eat at the Rainforest for less.

<u>Donald's Dining Safari At Tusker House</u> – If you want a much more laid back and relaxing character dining experience, you might check out Donald's character dining

experience at Tusker House. There are a variety of characters and some great American food options available on the buffet.

The Boma – We highly recommend that you take the short bus ride from the Animal Kingdom to the Animal Kingdom Lodge. The Lodge is absolutely stunning with lots to do and plenty to see. Warning, it will be difficult to walk around the lodge without ending up eating at the Boma restaurant; The smells are almost too much to resist.
This is another must if you have never experienced dining here. The buffet is loaded with a variety of African dishes, flavor filled soups, salads, meats and breads. Finish off your meal with one of many dessert options available on the buffet – We absolutely love the zebra domes.

After your meal, plan on spending some extra time exploring the lodge and viewing the giraffes, zebra's and other animals on the savannah. It can be a bit expensive to eat at the Boma if you are not on the meal plan. However, if you are on the meal plan, it will only cost you one table service allowance.

Animal Kingdom Snack Options

Tamu Tamu Refreshments – A large variety of snack options including a family favorite, Dole Whip ice cream. You can also grab an ice cream sundae here as well.

Kusafiri Coffee Shop and Bakery – Some of our favorite snack and Pastry options.

Dino Bites – Huge ice cream sandwich cookies that are big enough to split, floats, sundaes and pretzels.

Popcorn Stands – If your family likes popcorn, consider purchasing the refillable popcorn bucket for $10. It's refillable for your entire stay for $1.50 at any park. It pays for itself with a couple refills and it's a nice souvenir

Epcot Dining Options

Counter Service Options

The dining options available at Epcot are more extensive than any other park at Disney World. We will often hop over to Epcot for lunch or dinner just because there are so many options to choose from.

Though it's tough to be overly selective, our favorite Counter Service Options at Epcot are <u>Sunshine Seasons</u> within The Land in Future World West, <u>La Cantina de San Angel</u> in Mexico and <u>The Rose and Crown Pub</u> in United Kingdom.

One reason that it's so difficult to pick our favorites at Epcot is because there are food options within every country around the World Showcase.

If you have a favorite food type, we recommend that you choose to eat accordingly. We will give you additional recommendations for Epcot since there are so many options available.

We love the <u>Sunshine Seasons Grill</u> because it has the largest variety of food and dessert options along with free drink refills. We love the Salmon, the wood fired grill options and the large sandwiches. There is something at the Sunshine Seasons for just about any appetite.

If you like Mexican food, one of our favorites is La Cantina de San Angel. The tacos are delicious, and our kids love to share the nachos. Finish off your meal with an order of empanadas or a margarita if you prefer.

If you like fish and chips, you have to try The Rose and Crown Pub in the United Kingdom. Since our first fish and chips order a few years ago, we have revisited this stand many times. The smell keeps luring us in...

Kringla Bakeri Og Kafe – We will remind you of this place in the dessert section. However, the sandwiches here are large and tasty too. I especially enjoy the Club but sometimes I will switch it up and get the ham and apple.

The World Showcase – beyond the few mentioned above, the World Showcase is loaded with options to fit your taste. During the spring flower and garden festival the options multiply as stands representing foods from around the world are opened. Come hungry...

Some of our favorites are the Brats in Germany, the Sweet and Sour Chicken in China, the sushi in Japan (great outdoor atmosphere), the chicken and lamb wraps in Morocco and the barbeque in America.

Sit-Down Options (1 table service allowance)

Via Napoli in Italy – This is one of our favorite sit-down dining options at Epcot because of the great food and lively atmosphere. You truly feel like you are enjoying a wonderful Italian meal within the heart of Italy.

READY. SET. DISNEY

The wood fired pizzas are fantastic, but this restaurant also has a wide variety of great pasta options to choose from as well.

Once again, this restaurant can be both a romantic experience for couples and a fun time for kids. Ask for a seat by a window if one is available.

No reservation? Don't panic, reservations often open up the day before so keep checking for availability on The My Disney Experience App.

If you are unable to make a reservation, you can just show up around an hour or so before you would like to eat and put your name in, they can often fit you in if you are willing to wait for a bit.

<u>The Biergarten</u> – if you like German food and don't mind mingling with others in a fun festive environment, we recommend that you try the Biergarten restaurant in Germany. The food is excellent, and you can't help but leave in a better mood than when you arrive.

<u>Akershus Royal Banquet Hall</u> in Norway – This is our choice for the best princess character dining experience at Disney. Though it is outside the fantasy laden atmosphere of the Magic Kingdom, this character dining experience has its advantages.

The food buffet options are better, in our opinion, than some of the other character dining experiences and the atmosphere is much more relaxing and laid back. Also, since Epcot is not the first choice for most little ones, the princesses seem to have more time to spend with each child than at other character dining experiences.

La Hacienda -vs- San Angel – When choosing between these two Mexican restaurants we recommend San Angel. The meals are good at both but larger at San Angel and we like the atmosphere better as well.

Premium Options (2 table service allowances)

Le Cellier – One of the few restaurants that we have not eaten at throughout Disney, mainly because we are a bit stingy with our table service allotments and this restaurant takes two. It's very expensive, but those that we know who have eaten here rave about it. We are told that they serve the best steaks in Disney World, but I suppose you can be the judge of that.

Epcot Snack Options

Les Halles Boulangerie-Patisserrie in France – There are so many great desserts and pastries here. Hard to narrow it down since everyone in our family likes something different. Just go! We promise you will find something you like.

Also, the ham and cheese croissants are fabulous if you are looking for more of a savory snack option. We have often used our snack option and eaten these croissants for lunch.

Kringla Bakeri Og Kafe in Norway – Tons of great snack options here as well. We love the school bread and the crème horns.

READY. SET. DISNEY

Sunshine Seasons Grill in The Land in Furture World West – Large variety of cupcakes and pastry items. My girls love the strawberry shortcake.

Karamell-Kuche in Germany – Amazing melt in your mouth caramel popcorn, caramel covered apples and strawberries. Sooooo good.

Popcorn Stands – If your family likes popcorn, consider purchasing the refillable popcorn bucket for $10. It's refillable for your entire stay for $1.50 at any park. It pays for itself with a couple refills and it's a nice souvenir

Hollywood Studios Dining Options

Counter Service Options

Our choices for the best Counter Service Options at the Hollywood Studios are ABC Commissary on Commissary Lane, PizzeRizzo on Grand Avenue, Woody's Lunchbox in Toy Story Land and Sunset Ranch Market on Sunset Boulevard.

ABC Commissary – has a variety of food options including burgers, ribs, chicken, salads and seasonal options. We recommend eating here if you have a family or group with varied tastes

PizzeRizzo – Apart from Via Napoli at Epcot, this is our favorite pizza place in Disney World. Though Via Napoli is a notch better, it's hard to beat the counter service price of the pizza at PizzeRizzo. Add to that the benefit of free drink refills and you got one of the best counter service options at Hollywood Studios.

Woody's Lunchbox – This dining location will likely become a favorite counter service eating spot for your children, especially if they are pre-teens. The Raspberry and Chocolate Hazelnut lunch box tarts are delish, and BBQ Brisket Melts are filling and yummy too. Most picky kids will love the grilled cheese sandwich.

Sunset Ranch Market – This is actually several restaurants in the same general area. Kind of like a food court at the mall. Though there are extensive meal options available, not everything is offered at the same place. So, everyone may need to split up, grab what they want and meet back together to eat. We love this location because we can all get what we want and everyone's happy.

Sit-Down Options (1 table service allowance)

Mama Melrose's on Grand Avenue – This is another one of our favorite sit-down dining experiences at Disney World. Mama's is a less known gem tucked away from the crowds at the back of Hollywood Studios. Eating here feels like being in a small diner somewhere in the beautiful countryside of Italy.

The meals are large and delicious with a variety of Italian options. We enjoy eating at Mama's and splitting meals. This is a better option than spending a similar amount to get our own meals at a counter service somewhere else in the park. We love the Lasagna, Chicken Parmesan and Spaghetti and meatballs.

This is another restaurant that can be both a romantic experience for couples and a fun time for kids. Once again, No reservation? Don't panic, reservations often

READY. SET. DISNEY

open up the day before so keep checking for availability on The My Disney Experience App.

If you are unable to make a reservation, you can just show up at Mama's an hour or so before you want to eat and put your name in. They can usually fit you in if you are willing to wait for a bit.

50's Prime Time Café on Echo Lake – This is just a fun and lively place to eat. We prefer it over the Sci Fi Diner and it's much less expensive than The Brown Derby. If you are looking for good food at a descent price and can't get into Mama Melrose's, this is your best bet.

Premium Options (2 table service allowances)

The Hollywood Brown Derby – The food at the Brown Derby is very good but dollar for dollar we feel that there are better options for multiple table service allowances. We recommend eating at Mama Melrose's or the 50's Prime Time Diner and using another table service allowance elsewhere.

Hollywood Studios Snack Options

The Trolley Car Café on Hollywood Boulevard (Starbucks) – Tons of great snack options and of course…Starbucks coffee

Oasis Canteen on Echo Lake – We love their funnel cakes and their ice cream floats.

Hollywood Scoops on Sunset Boulevard – Excellent ice cream sundaes, hand dipped cones and ice cream cookie sandwiches

Popcorn Stands – If your family likes popcorn, consider purchasing the refillable popcorn bucket for $10. It's refillable for your entire stay for $1.50 at any park. It pays for itself with a couple refills and it's a nice souvenir

READY. SET. DISNEY

FIFTEEN

Our Top 10 Disney Dining Locations

We understand that this booklet is primarily geared toward saving money on your Disney vacation. However, we would like to mention a few of our very favorite dining locations at Disney World just in case you would like to have a splurge or two on your trip.

Though there many great restaurants at Disney Springs to choose from, we don't list many here because, though it is Disney property, it's more of a huge, super nice outlet mall than a true Disney experience.

We understand that in choosing from hundreds of available restaurants many will have preferences very different from ours, nevertheless, here are our top 10 with only a small regard to their pricing:

10) Akershus is a sit-down buffet in Norway at Epcot that offers a great variety of Norwegian flavors along with character greetings. We love the friendly service and the authentic Norwegian feel. The atmosphere here really makes you feel as if you are eating in a quaint Nowegian village,

READY. SET. DISNEY

9) Earl of Sandwich at Disney Springs has both great food and great pricing. Though Earl is not a fancy sit-down, the quality of the food and the overall value place it within our top 10. If you just want a super sandwich and snack at a great price, this is the place for you. I especially enjoy The Montague but there are a ton of options to choose from and free drink refills.

8) The Boathouse at Disney Springs overlooks the waterfront and has a nautical theme. This is a great day location with plenty of romantic seating along the waterfront. Disney Springs offers plenty to do after dinner as well. For your meal, we might suggest the Mahi-Mahi fish tacos. They are delicious. If you prefer, there are a great variety of steak options to choose from as well.

7) **Be Our Guest** (Belle's Castle) is a magical adventure in dining. Dinner at Belle's is served family style in very large portions. Eating a dinner meal at Be Our Guest is more expensive than eating lunch for sure, but the food is super good and the dining experience is exceptional. Though you will need to make reservations for lunch or dinner, lunch is still considered a counter service and dinner a table service. Choose to sit in the Library, the Ball Room or the Rose Room. The food is good, the atmosphere is even better.

6) **Via Napoli** has excellent food with the unique feel of eating on the street in Italy. We love the wood-fired pizzas. The atmosphere is very lively and fun. Though Via Napoli is known for its wood fired pizzas, there are a variety of Italian options to choose from. We recommend making reservations as early as possible since Via usually books months in advance. Excellent for the entire family.

5) Cinderella's Royal Table – Nothing quite beats the atmosphere of being inside of the Cinderella Castle. My girls were absolutely mesmerized by the wonder of being treated as princesses within the beauty of Cinderella's Castle.

Of course, if we were ranking on atmosphere alone, Cinderella's royal table would have been higher on our list. However, it is quite expensive, and the food is not quite as good as some others on our list.

4) Mama Melrose on Grand Ave at Hollywood Studios is a hidden gem away from the crowds of Hollywood Studios. Catch the feel of sitting in a local Italian diner with authentic Italian food. The portions are very generous, and the atmosphere is quaint, joyful and relaxing. Compared to the value of other deluxe Disney restaurants, Mama's comes out on top in our opinion.

Once again, when we are not on the meal plan, we love to make reservations at Mama Melrose's and split the meals.

We usually end up spending a little more than we would have at a counter service but, the food and atmosphere are way better and the we typically have plenty to eat.

3) The Rainforest Café and T-Rex have been a dining highlight for our family for many years. We include them together because they are both Landry restaurants with similar features. Though the themes are different (Rainforest animal's vs Dinosaurs and prehistoric animals) both have incredible atmosphere. The quality and variety of food options are great at both restaurants.

We recommend the Rainforest Café at the Animal Kingdom over the one at Disney Springs for sure. Disney Springs is way more crowded, especially on the weekends. The restaurant at the Animal Kingdom is larger and the service is much better in our opinion.

If you prefer dinosaurs to Gorillas and Elephants, you may want to try T-Rex at Disney Springs. Both restaurants are super amazing, and the food is similar at both places because both are Landry's restaurants. We love both but we go to the Rainforest more often because, once again, Disney Springs is way more crowded. Again, going online and grabbing a Landry's membership will pay off big time if you plan to visit either of these restaurants during your Disney vacation.

READY. SET. DISNEY

2) The Boma at the Animal Kingdom Lodge is simply amazing. This place is loaded with African culture and incredible food. The delicious African buffet coupled with the sights and sounds of Africa make this dining experience one of a kind. This has routinely been a family favorite over the years. We have gone for breakfast, lunch and dinner, all are very good, but dinner is by far our favorite time to visit.

1) Ohana at the Polynesian Resort is our favorite dining experience at Disney World. The combination of Polynesian atmosphere and the various kabobs cooked over an open fire pit and served family style make this restaurant the complete Disney experience.

There is entertainment throughout your dining adventure and if you time it right, you can watch the Magic Kingdom fireworks through the large glass windows as you dine.

The pineapple bread pudding with ice cream and butter rum sauce to top off your meal is one of our favorite desserts at Disney World.

Ohana – Our pick for Disney's #1 Dining Experience

NOTES

READY. SET. DISNEY

NOTES

NOTES

SECTION THREE

DISNEY DAILY GUIDE MAPS

READY. SET. DISNEY

SIXTEEN

EVERYTHING YOU NEED TO KNOW ABOUT DISNEY DAILY GUIDE MAPS

The Disney Daily Guide Maps are also available as individual pocket-sized booklets that you can carry with you through each of the Disney Parks. Many have found this format very helpful since they can access the information easily as they journey through each park.

What Are Disney Daily Guide Maps?

Over the years our family has helped other families and individuals to plan and prepare for their Disney vacations. Along the way, we have developed an approach or process of encountering each Disney park. We share this process with you within each of our Daily Guide Maps.

After 20+ years of doing Disney together as a family, we have gained a ton of insight and valuable information that we can share with your family. Our hope is that we can help others to experience the magic of Disney the way that we have through the years.

READY. SET. DISNEY

The Guide Maps were designed, after many years of trial and error, to help families to experience each Disney park without becoming frustrated and overwhelmed.

Daily Guide Map Structure

Each Guide Map begins with an overview of the park and some recommendations concerning rides, shows and attractions that you won't want to miss. Then there is a brief description and evaluation of each ride, attraction and show.

We then make Fast Pass suggestions and Dining recommendations with variations for children. The greatest tool within each Guide Map is the step by step process that we have developed for encountering each Disney park.

The Guide Maps take you through each portion of the day, morning, lunch, afternoon, dinner, evening and late evening – giving you secret tips and suggestions along the way. The Guide Maps can be a great tool to help make your Disney days a little less stressful and more enjoyable

The intent Of Disney Daily Guide Maps

The Daily Guide Maps are not intended to limit or confine your vacation, but to serve you when you're unsure how to approach each park. Following our seasoned advice can help make your Disney vacation a little more Magical.

Going to Disney World for the first time can be overwhelming and frustrating without a little guidance and direction. There will certainly be moments in your Disney vacation when you could use a bit of advice and / or direction. The Daily Guide Maps will be there for you in those moments.

If you choose to take a detour from a Guide Map from time to time, no worries. Again, the map is intended to give you guidance when you want it and not to limit your choices. The choices you make as you go through the day with your Guide Map will depend on the age of your children, your personal preferences and your budget.

We have also given our suggestions for value, sit-down and premium meal options within each Disney park. We hope that the tips and lessons that we have learned over the years will help remove the stress that you might otherwise feel as you encounter each Disney park for the first time.

We have outlined what we believe to be the most rewarding and stress-free way to encounter each Disney park, but they are only suggestions so treat them as such. If you find that you are unable to follow the schedule you can easily jump back into the Guide Map at any time and pick up where you left off.

How To Use The Daily Guide Maps

Begin by choosing one of the Daily Guide Maps and read through the Quick Overview, Highlights, Rides & Attractions sections. This will give you a general idea of the park and will begin to familiarize you with some of the ride

READY. SET. DISNEY

and attraction options available to you. Underline or highlight rides, attractions or shows that you find especially relevant to your vacation planning.

There is a "notes" page at the end of each section for you to jot down any additional thoughts or ideas that come to mind as you read through each section. This information will be helpful as you journey through each park.

After you have a general idea of everything the park has to offer, read through the Daily Guide Map sections one at a time. As you read, imagine going through each section of the park as the Guide Map describes. Highlight areas of the Map that are most useful and underline anything that you want to remember.

If there are changes that you would like to make to the Guide Map, you might want to note those changes in the margin. Be sure to make a note of any ideas that pop into your head and jot down any changes to the Guide Map on the note's pages at the end of each section.

We recommend that you read through each Daily Guide Map thoroughly before finalizing the dining and / or Fast Pass reservations for your trip. The Guide Map may highlight some information that may alter your dining or FP choices.

Above all, have fun dreaming with your loved ones about your upcoming Disney vacation. The rising anticipation about your trip is a huge part of the excitement

What We Love About Each Park

Magic Kingdom brings out the wonder and inner child in each of us. It stretches our imaginative energy beyond its normal limits. It reminds each one of us, regardless of age, that we have value and that we are princes and princesses (big or small).

Animal Kingdom awakens a sense of adventure in us and fosters an appreciation for the vast animal kingdom around us. In some way we are all a part of this wonderful creation.

Epcot brings the world together into one place. It inspires us to love and live-in unity with one another, to imagine a better tomorrow and to appreciate the greatness in the diversity of humanity.

Hollywood Studios celebrates the creativity that exists in each person and pushes us to pursue our dreams. We are each creative and genius in our own ways.

READY. SET. DISNEY

SEVENTEEN

THE MAGIC KINGDOM

MAGIC KINGDOM: A QUICK OVERVIEW

The Happiest Place On Earth – The Magic Kingdom, for most children, and a good number of adults, is quite possibly "the happiest place on Earth." The moment you enter the park and step onto Main Street USA and head toward Cinderella Castle, you will begin to comprehend the wonder and magic of this amazing place.

Where To Begin? – Despite the wonder of this place, deciding what to do at The Magic Kingdom and when to do it can be a bit overwhelming. This Guide Map should help you navigate through the myriad of options available to you. Relax, slow down and enjoy every moment. It's going to be a magical day.

Still Deciding When To Go? – If you are still deciding when to take your Disney vacation, we recommend that you choose to visit during a low season if possible. When choosing your Magic Kingdom day, we suggest that you choose a non-weekend day to visit this park – preferably Tuesday, Wednesday or Thursday.

READY. SET. DISNEY

Get Ready For A Magical Day - Weekend or weekday, no worries – you will have a great time anyway. We hope that the information in this book will be helpful in planning and preparing for your Disney vacation.

MAGIC KINGDOM HIGHLIGHTS

Fantasy Land - The Seven Dwarfs Mine Train is super fun. (Must be 38"), Peter Pan's Flight &, Winnie The Pooh are whimsical and a must for young children, Under The Sea – Journey of the Little Mermaid is one of our favorites in Fantasy Land and the age old classic It's a Small World (of course). Mickey's Philharmagic is just O.K.

Frontierland – Splash Mountain and Thunder Mountain Railroad are Highlights. Tom Sawyer Island is a relaxing excursion. Country Bear Jamboree is entertaining and funny.

Liberty Square – Older kids and adults may want to visit The Haunted Mansion. The family may also choose to take a lap around Tom Sawyer Island on the Riverboat.

Adventureland – The Jungle Cruise, Pirates of the Caribbean, Swiss Family Tree House, Aladdin's Carpets for the little ones.

Tomorrowland – Space Mountain is a must. Buzz Lightyear's Space Ranger Spin is one of our favorites as well. The Tomorrowland Speedway is a younger kid favorite. The Astro Orbiter is descent. For a more relaxing excursion hop on The People Mover, it doesn't get all the hype but we love it.

Top Notch Shows – There are a few shows that you will want to catch if possible. Mickey's Royal Friendship Fare at the Castle, the Move it! Shake it! Dance and Play it! Street Party and Enchanted Tales with Belle in Fantasyland.

Magical Adventures – There are also two fantastic interactive adventures that your children will love if you would like to include them in the magic of your day. The first adventure is Sorcerers of the Magic Kingdom which takes you throughout the MK in search of clues to defeat the evil villains.

The second is A Pirates Adventure where you collect treasure finder cards throughout Adventureland. These adventures will especially appeal to all pre-teen children.

READY. SET. DISNEY

RIDES AND ATTRACTIONS

The Seven Dwarfs Mine Train – Great theme, smooth ride, long lines. The reason the lines are so long is because most adults and children over 38" tall is love this ride. Unless you have a FP, stay away from the lines in the middle of the day. Instead, ride it when the park opens or during the firework show at night.

Under The Sea With Ariel – Very entertaining and fun. Most children will love this ride regardless of age. The atmosphere of the Grotto is amazing.

Peter Pan's Flight – Again, great theming that will capture your child's imagination. The Lines are often too long to wait without a FP unless you go first thing in the morning or later in the evening.

Winnie the Pooh – The younger ones will love this ride. Fun and whimsical. A classic...

Barnstormer – This is a fun little coaster that we have ridden dozens of times over the years. Lines can be a bit long because this is the only roller coaster children under 38" tall can ride.

Jungle Cruise – This is a great ride for the entire family to enjoy. The little ones may not catch all the little jokes, but they will appreciate the boat ride and beautiful scenery. This is another classic attraction that has been a family favorite through the years.

Pirates Of The Caribbean – This is another great ride that the entire family will enjoy. There's nothing too scary to frighten little ones. The atmosphere inside the pirate castle is incredible. Great time...

Swiss Family Tree House – Though there are a lot of steps to walk up, it's worth the effort. The imagination of your children will be carried away by thoughts of living in a giant tree. Warning: You may be challenged to build them a treehouse when you get home.

Country Bear Jamboree – Good show, lots of humor. You probably won't need to revisit this show every year, but it is worth seeing for a few good laughs.

Splash Mountain (40" and Over) – This may be the happiest attraction at Disney. The story and theming of the ride are super fun for all ages.

There is one larger plunge (50ft) but you won't get too wet unless you sit in the front row. On hotter days Disney tends to turn up the water works a bit.

Thunder Mountain Railroad (40" and Over) – Once again, it's the theme of the ride that makes it so incredible. You feel like you are on a mine train in the Old West. So much fun. Ride in the back for a wilder ride.

Tom Sawyer Island – The entire family will enjoy discovering the caves and trails on Tom Sawyer Island. It's a quick getaway from the crowds of Frontierland. This is a good place to have a picnic or to find a quiet spot and relax.

Haunted Mansion – Very well themed. A bit too scary for younger children. We don't ride it often, but it's a favorite for many.

The Riverboat – Great relaxing ride around Tom Sawyer Island. Also, you get to see a good bit of The Magic Kingdom from a different perspective.

Buzz Lightyear – Every member of your family will have fun hunting down Zurg and bringing peace back to the galaxy. We give some scoring tips later in this Guide Map.

READY. SET. DISNEY

Tomorrowland Speedway – You must be 52" tall to ride alone on this ride but little ones can ride along with an adult. They can even drive as long as they can push the gas.

Space Mountain – This is one of the most iconic rides at Disney World. Blast off into outer space on this one of a kind roller coaster ride in the dark.

The People Mover – If you want about a 10 to 15 minute break, the People Mover is a great option. This quick moving ride takes you behind the scenes of Tomorrowland. We really enjoy this relaxing ride.

Mickey's Royal Friendship Fare – This show at the castle main stage will captivate your children. It's definitely worth getting a good spot by the stage 10 to 15 minutes before show time. You will want to get as close to the stage as you can to see the characters...it's Magical.

Move It! Shake It! Dance and Play It! Street Party – Lively and fun with a full cast of Disney characters. Shows occur a few times during the day. We watch the show on the main stage and then stick around for the party to begin.

Disney's Festival of Fantasy Parade – This exciting tribute to Fantasy Land begins at the intersection of Adventureland and Frontierland and ends with a trip down Main Street USA. Plan on getting a good seat along the parade route about 20 minutes before the it begins.

Enchanted Tales With Belle – Sit with Belle as she entertains her guests by re-telling the story of Beauty and the Beast. Be careful, she may just choose you from the audience to take part in her story.

MAKING FAST PASS RESERVATIONS

In preparation for your Magic Kingdom day, we recommend that you book your Fast Passes as early as possible. The Fast Pass for Seven Dwarfs Mine Ride will be the most difficult to get so book the FP for this ride first. If you are staying at a Disney Resort, you will be able to make FP reservations <u>60 days</u> before your arrival date.

We recommend that you download the <u>My Disney Experience App</u> to make your FP reservations. Otherwise, you can call Disney customer service directly at 407.939.1284. If you wish to make Fast Pass reservations to coincide with this Guide Map, we recommend that you make the following Fast Pass reservations for your day at the Magic Kingdom:

FAMILIES WITH YOUNGER CHILDREN:

<u>For Early Morning Arrival</u>
Seven Dwarfs Mine Ride @ 11 am
Under The Sea @ 1 pm
Peter Pan's Flight @ 2 pm

<u>For Afternoon</u> Arrival
Seven Dwarfs Mine Ride @ 1 pm
Under The Sea @ 2 pm
Peter Pan's Flight @ 3 pm

<u>For Early Evening Arrival</u>
Seven Dwarfs Mine Ride @ 4 pm
Under The Sea @ 5 pm
Peter Pan's Flight @ 6 pm

FAMILIES WITH OLDER CHILDREN:

<u>For Morning Arrival</u>
Space Mountain @ 11 am
Thunder Mountain Railroad @ 1 pm
Pirates or Jungle Cruise @ 2 pm

READY. SET. DISNEY

For Afternoon Arrival
Space Mountain @ 1 pm
Thunder Mountain Railroad @ 3 pm
Pirates or Jungle Cruise @ 4 pm

For Early Evening Arrival
Space Mountain @ 4 pm
Thunder Mountain Railroad @ 6 pm
Pirates or Jungle Cruise @ 7 pm

Later Arrivals – If you plan to sleep in, relax by the pool or arrive even later to the MK for any reason, no worries. This Guide Map can still assist you as you make your way through the park. You will need to adjust your FP times and / or meal reservation times, but everything else should flow seamlessly.

Fast Pass Rules:

You can check in to use your Fast Passes 5 minutes before your start time and up to 75 minutes after your start time.

In other words, your fast passes are good for an hour from your start time, but they will still let you in up to 15 minutes after the hour is up.

If you miss your FP altogether, ask for mercy. Sometimes the attendants will allow you to ride anyway.

Don't Forget The Child Swap – Using the Child Swap throughout the day will allow parents the chance to ride some of the rides that their younger children are unable to ride.

How The Child Swap Works – Just go to the attendant at the entrance to the ride and ask for a Child Swap Pass. One parent waits in line with up to 2 older children.

After riding, the other parent rides with the older children without waiting in line. This allows both parents the opportunity to ride with up to 2 kids while only one parent has to wait in line.

The parent staying with the smaller children can head to another ride or grab a snack with the little ones until it is their chance to ride. If you have Fast Passes for the ride, no one waits long, it's a great deal all the way around.

READY. SET. DISNEY

MAKING DINING RESERVATIONS

The meal reservations that you make for this day will depend on your preference and your budget. If you choose lunch at Belle's, a sit-down meal or a character dining experience, you will want to make reservations as early as possible. You are permitted to make your reservations up to 180 before your check in date.

You are permitted to make meal reservations up to <u>6 months</u> prior to your arrival date. To coordinate with this Guide Map, consider making one or more of the following meal reservation suggestions:

<u>Breakfast</u> – Chef Mickey's or Park Fare

<u>Lunch</u> – Be Our Guest or Park Fare

<u>Dinner</u> – Ohana, Be Our Guest, Park Fare or Spirit of Aloha Luau

We understand that it is unlikely that you will choose 2-character meals and lunch at Belle's on the same day. That's a ton of food. Haha. Though I'm sure that some of you are up for the challenge, we only offer multiple meal suggestions to guide you in the various options from which you may choose.

Coordinate With The Guide Map When Possible - If your schedule permits, we recommend that you make meal reservations to coordinate with the suggested FP time selections in your Guide Map. We have made suggestions to coincide for both families with younger and older children, but you may choose a menu that favors the adults in your group if you prefer.

DISNEY
DAILY GUIDE MAPS

Magic Kingdom

READY. SET. DISNEY

EARLY MORNING

Why Not Eat Breakfast On The Go? – We suggest that you start your Magic Kingdom day by eating a quick breakfast in your room or a quick service meal at your resort or hotel. Magic Kingdom is opening earlier than it used to and this is the one park that an early arrival can be most beneficial.

Some may choose to eat breakfast at <u>Chef Mickey's</u> at the Contemporary Resort, <u>Park Fare</u> at the Grand Floridian or at another Disney restaurant. If so, we recommend that you make your breakfast reservations as early as possible.

When To Book Your Character Breakfast? – If you are set on having a character breakfast, we recommend that you consider booking one on a day that you will be going to Epcot or Hollywood Studios. There is already so much to fit in to your Magic Kingdom day and your day at Epcot and / or Hollywood Studios will likely be far less packed.

Want To Arrive Early? – It is very difficult to eat a buffet and still arrive at the Magic Kingdom 45 min or so before the park opens. If you choose to bypass the early entrance idea, Chef Mickey's or Park Fare would be great breakfast options to start your day!

Top Secret Park Entrance Tip - Many Disney visitors are unaware that the parks often open earlier than the published times suggest. You may want to plan on being at the gate at least 45 minutes before the park opens to beat the crowds and watch the entrance show.

READY. SET. DISNEY

Castle Entrance Show – There is an entrance show in front of the Castle that begins 30 minutes before the park opens. If you make it to the Magic Kingdom about 15 minutes before this show begins, you will be rewarded.

Be Our Guest – If you choose to bypass a large breakfast, we recommend that you make reservations to eat at Be Our Guest for lunch. You can make this reservation 6 months before your arrival date. If you are traveling during one of the busy seasons, this becomes even more important.

If you are on the meal plan, there is another benefit to eating at Belle's for lunch. Since Be Our Guest is a Counter Service option at lunchtime, you can use your sit-down at another restaurant for dinner if you have the meal plan.

Either way, Be Our Guest is one of the best counter service options at Disney. We hope that you have the opportunity to enjoy the magical atmosphere of eating in Belle's Castle while at Disney.

Top Secret Strategy Tip - If you make it to the gate when the park opens its best to head straight for the back of the park. It typically takes most people a bit before they can get back there so you may buy yourself a little time before the crowds move in.

For families with younger children, we recommend that you go straight to Fantasy Land or Storybook Circus and ride the rides that you won't have Fast Passes for later in the day. This would also be a great chance to hit a character greeting spot since the lines should be relatively short for at least the first hour after the park opens.

<u>Older kids and adults</u> may want to head for the larger attractions that they don't have Fast Passes for later in the day. Pick a land, Frontierland, Tomorrowland or Adventureland, and go for it.

Everyone should be able to hit 2 or 3 rides before the crowds set in. The Magic Kingdom typically gets very busy by 11 am (especially Fantasy Land) so you will want to head for lunch around that time and then use your Fast Passes.

If you are still stuffed from your character breakfast you may want to move lunch to a later time.

READY, SET, DISNEY

Notes

LATE MORNING

Your First Fast Pass - After hitting some of the attractions that you have no Fast Passes for, it's time to use your first FP sometime between 10.30 and 11.30.

If you are following our Fast Pass suggestions, families with younger children are headed to The Seven Dwarves Mine Ride and families with older children are headed to Space Mountain.

Of course, if you are arriving later in the day, you will need to adjust your FP times accordingly.

After this FP, families with younger children may choose to visit another attraction in Fantasy Land that they don't have a FP for later in the day. The Tea Cups and Under The Sea With Ariel are a couple of our favorites.

Families with older children may wish to visit one of the attractions in Tomorrow Land that they have no FP for later in the day. We recommend the Astro Orbiter or Buzz Lightyear. If you must choose one, go with Buzz. "To Infinity and Beyond"

Another great option if you have both younger and older children is The Tomorrowland Speedway. This attraction is between Fantasy Land and Tomorrow Land so it would be a great place to meet after everyone uses their Fast Pass.

Top Secret Scoring Tip – Wanna be a Galatic Hero at Buzz Lightyear's Ranger spin? After years of planetary piloting, we have discovered a few secrets. In the first room, aim for the target on the left arm of the robot on your left. When you see Zurg, aim for the target directly below him on his space scooter. You will score 100,000 points each time you hit one of these targets.

READY. SET. DISNEY

Note: You can check in to use your Fast Passes 5 minutes before your start time and up to 75 minutes after your start time.

In other words, your Fast Passes are good for an hour from your start time, but they will still let you in up to 15 minutes after the hour is up. If you miss your FP altogether, ask for mercy. Sometimes the attendants will allow you to ride anyway. Just put on a frown and have a good excuse ready! Most Disney workers can't handle sad faces and will let you in.

Head For The Castle – Alternatively, after you use your first FP you might consider heading to the Cinderella Castle main stage for Mickey's Royal Friendship Faire.

Check your Disney app or brochure to verify start times; they do change from time to time.

This show is great for all ages, but if you have older kids who might prefer another option, they may want to run over to Adventure Land and jump on Pirates of the Caribbean or The Jungle Cruise while the little ones catch the show at the Castle. You can check the wait times on your My Disney Experience App.

Get Pixie Dusted – On your way to the Castle Main Stage you might make a quick pit stop at the Bibbidy Bobbidy Boutique behind the Castle for a quick photo inside and to allow the fairy godmother to shower your little ones with pixie dust. A little pixie dust may do your older kids some good as well.

Stay For The Street Party – After the stage show you will be in a great position to watch the Move it! Shake it! Dance and Play it! Street Party at 11am.

Shows For All Ages – Both of these shows will be a big hit for most young children. Older children may bypass the stage show and street party and choose another option if they prefer.

However, we would guess that your older children will thoroughly enjoy these shows if they decide to stay. Our girls still love them even though they are "grown up." The magic is indifferent to age.

Did You Miss The Show? – If you miss either the stage show, or the street party, no worries, there will likely be others scheduled later in the day. Check the Times Guide for the times of shows later in the day.

READY. SET. DISNEY

Notes

LUNCH TIME

Still Stuffed? – If you have chosen to eat a huge breakfast, you may want to skip lunch, eat a snack or lighter lunch or pack some sandwiches. We usually get stuffed at breakfast buffets and aren't that hungry again until dinner.

Are You Starving? – If you have passed on the breakfast buffet and are ready to Chow Down, <u>Be Our Guest</u> is a great lunch option. Typically, you will need to make advanced reservations for Be Our Guest, so I hope you have done that. If you have no reservation, go to the check in window and see if they can squeeze you in.

Below, we have chosen our top 3 lunch options for both families with younger and older children. "*" denotes character dining experience. We have also included lunch options that may be preferable adults and some older children who would prefer to bypass a character dining experience.

Our Favorite Lunch Options (Young children)

Counter	Sit-Down	Premium
Be Our Guest	Park Fare *	Cinderella's Castle
Starlight Cafe	Chef Mickey's *	
Pinocchio Village Haus	Crystal Palace *	

Our Favorite Lunch Options (Older Children)

Counter	Sit-Down	Premium
Be Our Guest	Crystal Palace*	Cinderella's Castle
Pecos Bill's	Park Fare*	
Starlight Cafe	Tony's Town Square	

READY. SET. DISNEY

Our Favorite Lunch Options (Adults)

Counter	Sit-Down	Premium
Be Our Guest	Ohana	Cinderella's Castle
Pecos Bill's	Tony's Town Square	
Starlight Cafe	Liberty Tree Tavern	

If you are looking for a very nice place to eat but don't want to pay the high prices for a character dining buffet, our favorite options are Be Our Guest and Tony's Town Square Restaurant. You can order from the menu at each location and even split meals if you choose. This will not work for Be Our Guest at dinner time because dinner at Be Our Guest is a character dining experience.

Secret Tip Regarding Be Our Guest - We recommend making reservations 6 months ahead for Be Our Guest or any of the character dining experiences. However, if you are unable to find a reservation for the number in your party, just make a reservation for 1 or 2.

The attendants will typically allow you to check in with a larger party (within reason) as long as you have a reservation. We prefer the Library, but all 3 rooms are magical. Bonus: There are Free Refills at the self-serve drink stations too. Our girls like the Croque Monsieur and Mrs Potts Turkey Sandwich.

"Try the Grey stuff it's delicious…" The song doesn't lie. Haha. Stay away from the Lemon Cream Puff, It's dreadful…

Note: If you decide to leave the park for a character dining at the Grand Floridian or the Contemporary, you can just jump on the resort monorail at the park entrance.

Be careful not to accidently jump onto the regular monorail because it will take you to the parking lot and not the resorts. The resort monorail leaves the Magic Kingdom and goes clockwise making stops at The Contemporary Resort, The Ticket Center, The Polynesian Resort, The Grand Floridian Resort and then returns back again to The Magic Kingdom.

Lunch Hopper Option – Lunchtime can be a very busy time at the Magic Kingdom and the least busy time at Epcot. If you have hopper passes, you may choose to hop on the monorail from the Magic Kingdom to Epcot for lunch. Epcot has some of the best lunch options on Disney property and the monorail should not be too busy during this time.

At Epcot, you could grab food at The Land or one of the many dining locations in the World Showcase. The Restaurant section in Section 2 should help you make the right choice. After having a nice lunch at Epcot (If you choose to hop) you could return to the Magic Kingdom and continue following the Guide Map.

When To Hop? – Since your Magic Kingdom day will likely be the most congested day in your schedule, we recommend staying put at MK for the entire day. Hopping from one park to another seems better suited for your Epcot or Hollywood Studios day. However, you may decide to hop anyway so go for it! If you get "hopping" fever, there is a section below that will help you to decide where to Hop.

READY. SET. DISNEY

Notes

AFTERNOON

Families With Older Children

After lunch, it's time to use your Fast Pass for Thunder Mountain Railroad and then wait in line for Splash Mountain. Thunder is typically a little longer wait than Splash unless it is a blistering hot day. If the line lengths are similar, we prefer waiting in the Splash line.

Families With Younger Children

After lunch, it's time to use your Fast Passes for Under the Sea with the Little Mermaid and Peter Pan's Flight. After riding these two rides you can check the wait times for the other rides in Fantasy Land or you can head over to Storybook Circus and ride the Barn Stormer and Dumbo's Flying Elephants. These rides will not appeal to your older children, but toddlers usually love them.

This might be a good time to visit some of your kids favorite Disney characters. There are character greeting locations in various places, but the two primary locations are Storybook Circus and Mainstreet USA. Regardless of age, character greetings are a Disney tradition – Everyone must participate.

Pirates And Jungle Cruise – After riding these two rides you can head for Pirates of the Caribbean and use your last Fast Pass. If your FP is not available yet, wait in line for Jungle Cruise (unless the line is too long) and then ride Pirates.

The attractions in Adventure Land are great for families with both younger and older children because they are attractions that everyone will enjoy.

READY. SET. DISNEY

Swiss Family Tree House And / Or A Pirates Adventure – Now may be a great time to take a walk through the Swiss Family Tree House. This attraction will also appeal to adults and children of all ages.

Since you are already in Adventureland, you may also want to do <u>A Pirate's Adventure.</u> This adventure could be completed in less than an hour, faster if you move quickly. Your kids will love it, even the older ones.

Check For Additional Fast Passes – Next, you might consider riding some of the rides that you don't have Fast Passes for. You might also find a <u>Disney Kiosk</u>, scan your magic bands and see if there are any Fast Passes still available for the rides you haven't ridden yet.

Some Good Close By Options are It's a Small World, Seven Dwarfs Mine Ride for the older ones who haven't ridden yet (probably a long wait), Under the Sea, Haunted Mansion, Tom Sawyer Island, Peter Pan's Flight and The Tea Cups.

Notes

READY. SET. DISNEY

SOME BREAK AND HOPPER OPTIONS

By this time in the day, your kids may need a break. Actually, you may be the one needing a break. Haha. Here are a few options to consider...

Go Back To The Room Or Pool At Your Resort – If you are not up for a nap, why not relax at one of the Disney resort pools? You are not limited to your own resort either.

You might consider visiting a Disney resort that you aren't staying at to grab a snack and let the kids take a dip in the pool. This will not be possible at The Magic Kingdom area resorts because you need a resort wristband to enter the pool area.

You can take Disney transportation to any Disney resort from the Magic Kingdom. The Caribbean Beach resort has many pools to choose from. We also love the pool at The Animal Kingdom Lodge, but it takes a bit longer to get there on the Disney bus.

Explore Other Disney Resorts – We love to walk around the Grand Floridian, The Polynesian and The Wilderness Lodge. These 3 resorts border the Magic Kingdom, so you can get to any of them quickly by monorail or boat.

Though you won't be allowed to swim in their pools, these resorts are a blast to explore. If your kids are big enough, they might enjoy doing the scavenger hunt at the Grand Floridian. Just see the Bell Captain at the front desk for the clues. We have a special section in our **Ready. Set. Disney** book that will help you in deciding which resort to visit.

The walk from The Polynesian to the Grand Floridian is one of our favorites. The Wedding Pavilion between the Grand

Floridian and the Polynesian resorts is Magical and is often open to walk through. We highly recommend checking this place out on your walk from the Grand Floridian to the Polynesian.

Find A Quiet Place To Sit And Unwind – Yes, the Magic Kingdom can get crazy. However, there are a few places where you can get away from people and relax. We love to sit out of the way at the entrance to Adventure Land just across the bridge coming from the castle. Also, try taking a side street off of Main Street USA. There are some little-known eating areas there with a relaxing atmosphere away from the crowds. Grab a snack or a cold drink, find a table and catch your second wind. Tom Sawyer Island is another place that we go when we want to get away from the craziness.

Spend Some Time In The Hall Of Presidents – This is one attraction that is rarely busy, quite relaxing and more entertaining than many expect. Plus, the air conditioning and escape from the crowds will give you an opportunity to recuperate.

Ride The People Mover – Another great relaxation option is to Ride the People Mover in Tomorrow Land. Even if the line appears long, it moves very fast and the wait is usually not that long.

This ride is very relaxing and enjoyable. The route takes you get behind the scenes of many Tomorrowland attractions. It's a great way to slow down and take a break.

READY. SET. DISNEY

Notes

DINNER

Below, we have chosen our top 3 dinner options for families. We have included options for both families with younger and older children as well as choices for adults who prefer to bypass a character dining experience. "*" denotes character dining.

Ohana - Our absolute favorite family place to eat at Disney is Ohana at the Polynesian resort. We include it as a lunch and dinner option because it is easily accessible from the Magic Kingdom by taking the resort monorail.

Our Favorite Dinner Options (Young children)

Counter Service	Sit-Down	Premium
Starlight Cafe	Park Fare *	Cinderella's Castle *
Pinocchio Village Haus.	Ohana	Spirit of Aloha Luau
Pecos Bill's	The Crystal Palace *	

Our Favorite Dinner Options (Older Children)

Counter Service	Sit-Down	Premium
Starlight Cafe	Ohana	Cinderella's Castle *
Pecos Bill's	Park Fare*	Spirit of Aloha Luau
Pinocchio Village Haus	The Crystal Palace *	

Our Favorite Dinner Options (Adults)

Counter Service	Sit-Down	Premium
Starlight Cafe	Ohana	Cinderella's Castle *
Pecos Bill's	Liberty Tree Tavern	Spirit of Aloha Luau
Pinocchio Village Haus	Tony's Town Square	

We recommend making reservations weeks ahead for **Ohana at the Polynesian Resort**. This is our favorite restaurant at Disney though it is a bit expensive without the meal plan. If you would

READY. SET. DISNEY

rather favor the kids for dinner you might consider a character dining experience at The <u>Crystal Palace</u>, <u>Park Fare</u> at The Grand Floridian Park Fare) or <u>Chef Mickey's</u> at The Contemporary.

The Spirit of Aloha at the Polynesian Resort is great entertainment for the whole family with great food. Each of these will require an advance reservation. The Cinderella's Royal Table is quite expensive, and you will need to book it 6 months before your trip. Both of these premium dinner experiences will cost two meal allowances if you are on the Disney Dining Plan.

If you want to watch the fireworks from the castle, you should make your meal reservations at least 30 minutes before the fireworks are scheduled to begin. Booking this time at the Castle is very difficult, but we are confident that you can pull it off if you remain persistent.

Notes

READY. SET. DISNEY

EARLY EVENING

Recharged? – When you are recharged and ready to go, head back to The Magic Kingdom (if you left) and ride the rides you missed.

HAVE YOU DONE EACH OF THESES?

Tomorrow Land – The People Mover, The Laugh Floor. We usually pass on Stich's Great Escape and The Carousel of Progress. The Carousel of Progress is worth seeing once for the sake of Disney history, but then you should be good for a while.

Fantasy Land – The Seven Dwarfs Mine Ride, Peter Pan's Flight, Under The Sea, Mickey's PhilharMagic, The Many Adventures of Winnie the Pooh, Mad Tea Party (Tea Cups).

We never leave without riding *It's a Small World*, it's just a tradition that we can't seem to shake

Frontier Land – The Country Bear Jamboree, The River Boat and Tom Sawyer's Island.

Main Street USA – Again, If you haven't caught Mickey's Royal Friendship Faire at Cinderella's Castle or the Move it! Shake it! Dance and Play it! Street Party on Main Street. Check your My Disney Experience app for show times. Both shows will add joy to your day.

Hopper Option – If you have a hopper pass option on your ticket and you want a change of pace from the Magic Kingdom, we suggest hopping over to Epcot or Hollywood Studios. These are a couple of our favorite parks at night and both are quick "hops" from the Magic Kingdom.

At Epcot you could walk around the World Showcase and then watch illuminations.

At Hollywood you could watch The Frozen Sing Along and end the day by watching the Star Wars Firework Show.

READY. SET. DISNEY

Notes

LATE EVENING

The Fireworks Show - If you have made it to this point, WAY TO GO!!! Just hang in there for the fireworks. It is not essential to be directly in front of the Cinderella Castle for the fireworks. We prefer a little back from the castle but still on Main Street. The closer you get to the castle, the more condensed the crowd becomes.

Another great place to watch the fireworks is from the Plaza View Terrace. If you get there early enough you can grab a table and sit through the fireworks. If the kids are tired and you want to get a quick exit to the Monorail after the fireworks, watch them near Town Hall. The view is still good, and you will beat the exiting crowds.

Top Secret Attraction Tip #1 – If you are still energized and want to bypass the firework show this time around, this would be a great time to visit a couple attractions that you have missed. Frontier and Adventure Lands are somewhat deserted during the fireworks.

This might be a great chance to take advantage of the **low wait times**. Even the wait time for the 7 Dwarves Mine Ride will go down drastically just before and during the fireworks. Of course, the lines for character greetings decrease drastically later in the day as well. This is probably because most little ones and their parents are too pooped out by this time to wait in long lines.

If you are attending Magic Kingdom on an evening that the park is open after the fireworks, you may choose to visit more attractions after the show. Apart from Friday and Saturday nights, this is typically one of the least busy times to visit the attractions. However, with little ones, I'll bet you will be ready to head for the exit. There's no shame in that! It's been a long day!

READY. SET. DISNEY

Top Secret Attraction Tip #2 – If there is an attraction that you haven't been able to ride because Fast Passes were unavailable, and / or the lines were too long, there is a trick. If you are able to stick it out until just before the park closes, get in line 5 minutes before the park closing.

When the park closes, all FP returns will end. The line for every ride is typically cut in half (at least). As long as you are in line before the park closes, you will not be turned away. The posted times are often longer than the actual wait time at this point in the evening.

We have done this for many rides at Disney like – The Seven Dwarfs Mine Ride, Space Mountain, Avatar Flight of Passage, Frozen Ever After, Soarin, Test Track, Toy Story Mania, Rockin Roller Coaster and The Tower of Terror. It usually works really well.

Top Secret Halloween Tip - Here is a good tip if you plan to attend one of the holiday parties at the Magic Kingdom – Mickey's Not So Scary Halloween Party or Mickey's Very Merry Christmas Party. Though these parties do not begin until 7 pm, you can enter the park at 4 pm and begin using your Fast Passes. Fast Passes cannot be used (after 7 pm) once the parties begin.

Top Secret Fireworks Tips – If you want to watch the firework show outside of the Magic Kingdom and want to find a good location, here's what we recommend.

The California Grill at The Contemporary Resort has a great view of the fireworks and they play the music over their speaker system. However, you will need dining reservations during the fireworks to take advantage of this tip. You can also watch the fireworks from <u>the boat docks at the Grand Floridian</u> and the <u>Disney Transportation and Ticket Center</u>. These places are rarely crowded and offer the added atmosphere of seeing the fireworks reflected off the lake.

How About A Little Romance? A <u>very romantic option</u> for watching the fireworks is <u>on the beach at the Polynesian Resort</u> or between the Polynesian and the Grand Floridian. If you have a blanket to lay out on the sand, it's even better.

Though you will not be able to see the elaborate movie presentation on the Cinderella Castle, watching the fireworks at one of these locations outside of the Magic Kingdom can be a wonderful and unique experience.

After the Fireworks - If you still have energy, you may choose to head back to your resort and take a late-night dip in the pool. If you prefer, you might choose to soak in the hot tub if your hotel or resort has one available. Another option is to jump in bed and watch a good Disney Movie as you drift off to sleep.

Record Your Memories - One last thing - make sure to keep a journal beside your bed to record the most memorable events of each day. Looking back on these memories after your trip will help you to relive the magic of your trip over and over again.

READY, SET, DISNEY

Notes

EIGHTEEN

HOLLYWOOD STUDIOS

HOLLYWOOD STUDIOS: A QUICK OVERVIEW

Hurrah For Hollywood – Each Disney park is uniquely themed and magical in its own way. Hollywood Studios combines the art of film making with the wonder and creativity of everything Disney. There is so much to see and experience at each Disney park and Hollywood Studios is no different. We are often asked: "which park do you like the most?" Our answer is typically: "We love them all the same but for different reasons."

Where To Begin?

Though you can easily spend the full day at Hollywood Studios (especially with the new additions), it is also possible that you may wish to take a break sometime in the course of your day. If this is the case, we will give you some relaxation suggestions to consider...

Need Some Down Time? = We suggest that, if you want some down time during your vacation, that you plan on taking part of your Epcot or Hollywood day to account for a little R & R. Recently, Hollywood has exploded with the addition of two new lands (Toy Story and Star Wars) so your Epcot day may be the best choice for including a little R and R but Hollywood is still a good choice as well.

READY. SET. DISNEY

Also, you might consider scheduling lengthy dining options, including character meals, on these days rather than scheduling them on your Magic or Animal Kingdom days.

Fun For Everyone – We have also included a few options and ideas for the younger children in your family as well (just in case). Disney has developed attractions that appeal to all ages and have also created the "Child Swap" to allow the adults to participate in some of the bigger rides. We will explain the details a bit later in this booklet.

MAGIC KINGDOM HIGHLIGHTS

Hollywood Studios has increasingly become a family favorite. With the opening of Toy Story Land this past year and Star Wars: Galaxy's Edge this past Fall, Hollywood Studios has become the new "hot" park to visit.

In this section, we highlight some of the top rides and attractions throughout Hollywood Studios. Later in the itinerary sections we make recommendations specific to both families with younger and older children.

SOME MUST SEE SHOWS

Hollywood Studios is as much about great shows as it is about great rides and attractions. For most of these shows you will not need to take out a FP as long as you arrive 20 to 30 minutes before the scheduled show time.

The exception to this rule might be <u>For the First Time in Forever</u> on a very busy day or if you want to guarantee an excellent seat. Otherwise, we recommend that you save your Fast Passes for some of the other attractions we will suggest in this Guide Map.

For the First Time in Forever – This is a super fun sing along. The comedians are very funny, and the songs are entertaining. Your little ones will absolutely love it, but I'll bet you will love it too. Don't miss this show if possible.

The Indiana Jones Epic Stunt Spectacular is another must see, action packed adventure that will appeal to all ages. There are some live dramatic scenes and a good bit of humor. Though the arena is large, this show can fill up quickly on a busy day. Consider arriving at least 20 minutes before show time.

Disney Junior Live on Stage – For your younger children, who love Disney Junior, this may be the highlight of their Disney vacation. Sing, dance and play with Disney Junior Pals in this live on-stage production.

Walt Disney Presents – If you are an avid Disney fan you might want to catch this short film. This show is a great overview of Walt's life and the process of Imagineering Disney Land and Disney World. It's very interesting if you would like to know more about the behind the scenes history of "The Happiest Place on Earth."

Beauty & the Beast Live on Stage – Join an entire cast of Beauty and the Beast characters for this live on-stage presentation. If you love the story of Beauty and the Beast, you won't want to miss this live version.

READY. SET. DISNEY

Muppet Vision 3D – This is a humorous show with some eye-popping 3D affects. It's appealing to all ages. Usually a short wait time so don't worry about getting a FP for this one.

Voyage of the Little Mermaid – Experience the highlight scenes of The Little Mermaid story in this live and animated presentation.

Street Shows – If you are walking down one of the Main streets at Hollywood and happen to see a show taking place, we recommend that you stop and watch. These shows happen at random times, but they are almost always super funny and entertaining. Stop and watch…

RIDES & INTERACTIVE ADVENTURES

Star Tours (40" and Taller) – Board Star Tours for a galactic adventure. You never know where you are going or what adventure you will encounter along the way. Lots of fun!

Toy Story Mania – This is a moving life-size version of some popular carnival games. Everyone in the family will have fun with this 4D shooting game. Don't miss it, especially if you have kids.

Mickie and Minnie's Runaway Railway – This is a super fun high adventure ride that all ages will enjoy. The special effects in this high-tech train ride will make this ride a highlight for many. Though it is very entertaining, the little ones can ride with no problem.

Slinky Dog Dash – This is a super fun new rollercoaster in the new Toy Story Land. Anyone over 38" can ride so many toddlers will be able to enjoy this ride as well. It's usually crazy busy so get the FP if you prefer this to other options in Tier 1.

Alien Swirling Saucers – Great theme and lots of fun for the little ones who are unable to ride some of the larger rides. The older kids may enjoy it but they won't be overly impressed.

Rock 'n' Roller Coaster – "Blast off in a stretch limousine through the freeways of Los Angeles to the rockin' tunes of Aerosmith." It's fast, smooth and awesome. The theming and interactive nature of this ride is hard to beat. Catch it while you can, we hear this ride won't be around much longer. Don't miss it!

Twilight Zone Tower of Terror (40" and Taller) – What an amazing theme. Disney does a terrific job of creating an entire story around this tower. The ride is an adventure that you can't miss. Unless, of course, you're scared!

Lightning McQueen's Racing Academy – This is a must see for little ones who love the Cars movie. The show is entertaining, funny and interactive. The wait times aren't usually long (especially for a new attraction) and everyone in the family will enjoy the show.

Jedi Training: Trials of the Temple – Watch as young Jedi fighters are trained to be the next generation of defenders of the galaxy. A select number of young Jedi fighters will

READY. SET. DISNEY

participate in the training. Visit the Indiana Jones Adventure Outpost early in the day to register your young Jedi for training.

Millennium Falcon: Smugglers Run – This is a much more interactive version of Star Tours. The fate of the Millennium Falcon actually rests, to some extent, in the hand of those piloting the ship. It's a lot of fun, but more so for the pilot and the gunner which are the front two seats.

Star Wars: Galaxy's Edge - The Rise of the Resistance – This may be the best attraction at Disney, but you will need a little extra ambition to participate, especially on busy park days.

In order to participate you need to show up when the park opens and log into the My Disney Experience App. Click on the Star Wars: Galaxy's Edge link and join a boarding group. The app will guide you through the process. You will be assigned a group and then must return later in the day to ride as the app specifies.

It is absolutely worth the extra effort, especially if you are a big Star Wars fan. In our opinion, this is the most high-tech and interactive ride at Disney and that's saying a lot!

On this attraction you will join the resistance on a secret mission and will be confronted and captured by the First Order. You will encounter a slew of Star Wars heroes and villains along the way. It's incredible.

Character Greetings – There are a variety of character greeting spots at Hollywood Studios and the wait times are typically far less than wait times at the Magic Kingdom.

Meet <u>Olaf</u> @ Celebrity Spotlight at Echo Lake. Meet <u>Mickey and Minnie</u> in Red Carpet Dreams on Commissary Lane.

Meet <u>Mike and Sully at Walt Disney Presents</u> and <u>Darth Vader</u> in Animation Courtyard. Meet an entire cast of <u>Toy Story characters</u> @ Pixar Place.

Meet <u>Star Wars Heroes and Villains</u> @ the Star Wars Launch Bay in Animation Courtyard.

It's always a good idea to visit the characters early in the morning or late in the day if you want to cut down on your wait time.

NIGHTTIME SHOWS

Fantasmic – Join Sorcerer Mickey in his epic battle with Disney Villains. A dynamic display of lazer lights, fireworks and special effects. The seating matters for this show so you may wish to show up at least 30 minutes early or grab a FP for this show on busy days.

Star Wars: A Galactic Spectacular – A great way to end the evening at Hollywood Studios. Relive the Star Wars Saga with fireworks, lazers and some giant film footage. Be sure to be somewhat central to get a good view of the movie screens. Too close can be a bit too loud and you get a better view of the screen if you aren't right up next to it.

READY. SET. DISNEY

MAKING FAST PASS RESERVATIONS

Book Your Fast Passes - In preparation for your Hollywood Studios day, we recommend that you book your Fast Passes as early as possible. So 60 days if you are staying on Disney property, 30 days otherwise.

You will definitely want to sign up <u>for The Rise of the Resistance</u> using the My Disney Experience app if you wish to participate in this attraction. Registration for this attraction usually begins at exactly 7 a.m. This attraction is often full **5 seconds** after registration begins. So be on the app and ready at 7 a.m.

The Fast Pass for <u>Slinky Dog</u> will be the most difficult to get so book the FP for this ride first especially if you have small children who are tall enough to ride (38").

Hollywood has recently changed the FP rules and now only allows 1 FP in Tier which includes: <u>Slinky Dog Dash</u>, <u>Toy Story Mania</u>, <u>Alien Swirling Saucers</u>, <u>Rock 'N' Roller Coaster</u> <u>and Tower of Terror</u>. The FP you choose will likely involve the age of your children and your enjoyment with thrill rides.

Remember, If you are staying at a Disney Resort, you will be able to make Fast Pass reservations <u>60 days before your arrival date.</u> We recommend that you download the <u>My Disney Experience App</u> to make your FP reservations. Otherwise, you can call Disney customer service directly at 407.939.1284.

Lines are unavoidable at Hollywood, especially if you want to ride multiple rides in Tier 1 (which most do). However, after choosing your best option from Tier 1, choosing two options from the remaining Tier may help. Here is a little advice on which to choose:

Star Tours – The wait time is not usually that long but it might be your best option for a FP outside of Tier 1

Fantasmic - If you plan to see this show and it's a super busy day, this show does fill up fast. Plus, the FP does help you get good seats which is rather important for this show.

For The First Time In Forever – This show is super funny and entertaining for children and adults. Though you will likely get into the theatre if you arrive 15 to 20 minutes before show time, if you want great seats, get the FP.

Disney Junior Dance Party – Also fairly easy to get in if you arrive early but if this is a must for your child you might want to grab a FP.

Beauty and the Beast Live On Stage – If you want to see this show, it's a good idea to either show up 20 to 30 minutes early (depending on the crowd) or grab a FP.

Indian Jones Epic Stunt Spectacular – This show has a huge seating capacity so its very likely that you will get seated if you come 10 to 20 minutes early. However, if you want good seats or want the chance of participating live on stage, grab the FP.

READY. SET. DISNEY

Disney's Early Morning Magic – We would have recommended this breakfast experience in Toy Story Land, it is quite a wonderful opportunity, but it comes at a cost. This is not just a breakfast but is an early pass to enjoy the attraction in Toy Story Land. If you wanna splurge a little, Go For It!

There is a separate entrance fee in addition to the cost of breakfast. If your kids are big Toy Story fans, this is something you might consider. The current cost is $79 for adults and $69 for kids age 3 to 9.

Fast Pass Rules – Again, you can check in to use your Fast Passes 5 minutes before your start time and up to 75 minutes after your start time. In other words, your Fast Passes are good for an hour from your start time, but they will still let you in up to 15 minutes after the hour is up.

If you miss your Fast Pass altogether, ask for mercy. Sometimes the attendants will allow you to ride anyway.

Don't Forget The Child Swap – If mom and dad want to use a Child Swap and ride a couple of the bigger rides at Hollywood Studios, we recommend <u>Rock 'n' Roller Coaster</u>, <u>Twilight Zone Tower of Terror</u> and <u>Toy Story Mania</u>.

The Child Swap – This pass will allow both parents to ride with up to 2 kids while only one parent waits in line. The parent staying with the smaller children can head to another ride or grab a snack with the little ones. Got a FP, no one waits long, it's a great deal.

Reconsider Your FP Options – We recommend if you have both older and younger children that you choose your FP options based more on your older children since the wait times for their rides are typically much longer. Even if you also have only younger children under 40" tall you may wish to wait in line for their attractions and use your FP options for mom and dad. This is where the Child Swap comes in handy.

Many of the attractions for younger children such as Disney Junior Live and Voyage of the Little Mermaid will likely be a minimal wait without a FP if you arrive a little early. Therefore, you may consider using your FP options to reserve larger rides where the lines are much longer. The exception might be Alien Swirling Saucers which at times can have significant wait times.

MAKING DINING RESERVATIONS

The meal reservations that you make for this day will depend on your preference, whether you have the meal plan and your allotted budget.

You are permitted to make meal reservations up to 6 months prior to your arrival date. To coordinate with this Guide Map, consider making one or more of the following meal reservation suggestions:

Breakfast – Disney Junior Play 'n' Dine or Disney's Early Morning Magic

Lunch – 50's Prime Time Café

Dinner – Mama Melrose

Though it is unlikely that you will choose 2 sit-down meals and a character dining option on the same day, we only offer meal suggestions to guide you and not to restrict your options.

READY. SET. DISNEY

We chose Disney Junior because it's really great for toddlers and younger children. Again, if you want a more complete morning option, try Disney's Early Morning Magic. Though it is a bit pricy, you receive early park entrance, a good breakfast and access to the attractions in Toy Story Land with little or no waiting.

We will explain our choices for lunch and dinner later in your Guide Map. We recommend that you make meal reservations to coordinate with the suggested Fast Pass time selections in your Guide Map if possible.

DISNEY
DAILY GUIDE MAPS

Hollywood Studios

READY. SET. DISNEY

EARLY MORNING

Later Arrival? - Once again, if you are planning some down time, a day of exploring or an extended dining experience, this day or your Epcot day might be a good choice for later entrance to a park. If you have gotten into a group for Galaxy's Edge, be sure to keep an eye on the app to make sure you are back in time to join the Resistance with your group.

This day may be a good opportunity to take advantage of some of the free fun highlighted earlier in Section 1 of this book. If you decide to eat at a breakfast buffet or sleep in a bit, just choose the later Fast Pass options.

Breakfast Anyone? - If you decide that you would like to kick start your day with an amazing breakfast, may we suggest that you make early breakfast reservations at <u>Disney Junior Play 'n' Dine</u>. You can join the Disney Junior Pals as they host this musical meal.

Disney's Early Morning Magic is a great option for those who want an early entrance to the park, a good breakfast and access to several Toy Story Land attractions with little or no waiting.

If neither of these options appeal to you, you may want to have breakfast on the go or reserve an alternate dining experience.

Begin By Registering For Star Wars: Galaxy's Edge and / or Jedi Training Registration

If you are planning to arrive early to the park and want to participate in the Galaxy's Edge attraction, make sure to register at the exact time the registration is made available on the My Disney Experience App (typically 7 a.m.) Once you are registered, you will be assigned a group number. Once your group number is called, you will have a 2-hour window to return for your adventure.

Also, if you plan to arrive early and your child would like to participate in Jedi Training: Trials of the Temple, we suggest that you begin your day by registering for Jedi training later in the day. You can register at The Indiana Jones Adventure Outpost at Echo Lake.

Star Tours and Muppet Vision 3D – After registering for Star Wars Galaxy's Edge and The Jedi training (if you choose to do so), Muppet Vision and Star Tours are right around the corner Muppet Vision is typically a relatively short wait and Star Tours is often a relatively short wait as well. If you have a FP for Star Tours, even better.

READY. SET. DISNEY

Notes

LATE MORNING

Depending on your preference or the preference of your children, you may choose to work your way through Star Wars: Galaxy's Edge or head straight to Toy Story Land.

Waiting in line for the Millennium Falcon would be your main choice if you decide to hang out at Galaxy's Edge for a bit.

If you have not visited Galaxy's Edge on a prior visit, you will want to allow some time just to look around and soak in the scenery. It's an unbelievable land to explore.

If you have a FP for Toy Story Mania, Slinky Dog Dash or Alien Swirling Saucers, keep your eye on the time. You will have up to an hour after your FP time begins to make it to the attraction. Usually there's a 15 minute grace period.

Toy Story Land – After Star Wars, you can proceed directly into the back entrance of Toy Story Land. Here you can use your Fast Pass to Toy Story Mania, Slinky Dog Dash or Alien Swirling Saucers if you chose one of these as your Tier 1 option. You may also choose to wait in line if you have not. Keep in mind, you may return to this land later in the day (just before park closing) and wait in line for one of these attractions if the lines are too long at this point.

I

f you have children, this may be a good time to meet a few of the Toy Story Characters. Apart from Star Wars, this is the newest addition to Hollywood Studios, and you will likely find it a bit congested. However, this is one of the most exciting areas for most children and many adults who have never grown up.

READY. SET. DISNEY

For The First Time in Forever – After visiting Toy Story Land, if you still have time before lunch, head over to the Frozen sing along – <u>For The First Time in Forever</u>. This will be a big hit for the entire family. If you are too hungry, go to Frozen after lunch…but <u>don't miss it</u>. This is a good FP choice if you want great seats and the park is a bit crowded.

Jedi Training – If your child registered for Jedi Training earlier in the day and is scheduled to report back to Echo Lake, keep track of the time so you don't miss your time slot. Also, pay attention to the progression of groups for Galaxy's Edge: Rise of the Resistance if you have registered for a group. This information will be on your My Disney Experience App.

Secret Tip Regarding Shows At Disney: When you are going to see one of the larger shows at Disney don't be the first to enter the auditorium. Those who enter first must file all the way across the row and get stuck on the far end. Instead, let some people in before you (not too many) and you will be seated closer to the center of the auditorium.

Notes

READY. SET. DISNEY

LUNCH TIME

Still Stuffed? – We suggest, if you choose to eat a large breakfast, that you consider skipping lunch or eating a lighter lunch at one of the counter service options.

There is also a great snack place on Echo Lake called the <u>Oasis Canteen</u> where you could grab a Funnel Cake, an Ice Cream or an Ice Cream Float.

In a hurry? Try ordering your food ahead on the My Disney Experience App. It will be waiting for you when you arrive at the counter.

Using the mobile app to get your food quickly is a great option if the park is packed however, we have discovered that some of our greatest memories occur when we slow down, take a break and enjoy our meal time with each other. So take it slow and enjoy your meals together whenever you can.

Starving? – If you have skipped breakfast and need a heartier meal for lunch, there are many restaurant options to fit your taste and budget at Hollywood Studios

Below, we have chosen our top 3 lunch options for families with small children. "*" denotes character dining experience.

Our Favorite Lunch Options (Older children)

<u>Counter</u>	<u>Sit-Down</u>	<u>Premium</u>
PizzeRizzo	Mama Melrose *	Brown Derby
ABC Commissary	50's Prime Time Café'	
Backlot Express	Sci Fi Diner	

Explaining Our Picks – We chose PizzeRizzo because the pizza is really good, its close by, there are free drink refills and kids typically love pizza.

We chose ABC Commissary because it is centrally located and has a large variety of options for both kids and adults. We chose Backlot Express because it is one of our favorite places to eat outside at Hollywood. The food is good too.

We chose Mama Melrose because It's one of the best restaurants at Disney with a great atmosphere and great food. We chose 50's Prime Time Café because it is a fun and vibrant atmosphere and is the next best choice to Mama's.

We chose The Sci Fi Diner because it has a unique atmosphere, and the food is good. See our comments on The Brown Derby in the dinner section.

Secret Tip regarding Mama Melrose – Mama Melrose is one of our favorite places to eat at Disney World. The atmosphere is charming and happy. It may not be the first choice for younger children, but there are a variety of options for kids and mom and dad will love it.

If you are not on the meal plan, Mama's can be a bit pricey if everyone orders a full meal. Thankfully, the meals at Mama's are large enough to split.

We love to eat here and split meals. This way we get a super meal at a sit-down restaurant for just a little more than the cost of a counter service.

Mama's is open for lunch and dinner so why not take a break and relax at one of the coolest restaurants at Disney. You will want to plan ahead and get reservations for Mama Melrose as soon as possible - especially for a dinner reservation.

READY, SET, DISNEY

Notes

AFTERNOON

Hopper Options – Since Hollywood Studios is close to Magic Kingdom and Epcot, it is entirely possible to hop to one of these parks if you prefer a change of pace. Hollywood and Epcot are connected by boat so taking a boat trip may be added fun for the kids as well as a relaxing break for you.

Also, the new Disney Skyliner connects Hollywood Studios to the Caribbean Beach Resort, The new Riviera Resort, Pop Century, Art of Animation and Epcot. You may choose to hop to one of these resorts or Epcot for lunch or dinner. Each of these resorts are beautiful and relaxing if you want some quality down time. The Skyliner is wonderful and scenic. It's quick, quiet, comfortable and usually not crowded.

Hop to Hollywood Later - You might consider starting your day at Magic Kingdom or Epcot and coming to Hollywood later in the day. You are only allowed to have Fast Passes at one park per day, so just choose later Fast Pass times for the rides at Hollywood.

Hop From Hollywood Later – Another option would be to arrive early at Hollywood and shoot over to The Magic Kingdom or Epcot later in the day to catch the Fireworks Show or Epcot Forever. Either way, you should be able to maximize your Fast Passes at Hollywood Studios while taking advantage of a few of your favorite attractions at another park earlier (or later) in the day.

Other Break Options - If you would like a break sometime during your Hollywood day, there are a ton of free or almost free options to choose from. We have outlined a variety of

READY. SET. DISNEY

recreational alternatives to being at a park earlier in Section 1 of this book. Hopefully you will find some good ideas to help you unwind a bit. There is so much more to the World of Disney than the four theme parks.

Find a quiet place to sit and unwind – One of our favorite places to sit and unwind is in the large seating areas at the Backlot Express. Another great option would be at the Baseline Taphouse on Grand Avenue. Grab a snack or a cool drink take a break for a bit. It always seems to help us gain our second wind.

Walt Disney Presents – Another relaxing way to unwind while also receiving an education is to visit Walt Disney Presents in Animation Courtyard. The film on the life of Walt Disney is interesting and educational. Also, there are several exhibits to visit with some of the friendliest cast members we have met at Disney there to answer your questions.

Notes

READY. SET. DISNEY

LATE AFTERNOON

No Hop, No Break? – If you decided not to hop to Epcot or Magic Kingdom and you have stayed the course at Hollywood, you will likely have time for a couple additional attractions before dinner.

Star Wars: Galaxy's Edge: If you registered for a group, keep checking the progression of the groups on your App to make sure you don't miss your window

Indiana Jones – Why not head back over to Echo Lake for the Indiana Jones Epic Stunt Show Spectacular? This show is packed full of action and humor. Plus it's relaxing and shaded. Kind of a break after all…

Star Tours – This might be a great time to visit Star Tours if you missed it earlier. This attraction is exciting and a must for all Star Wars fans. If you have chosen to get a FP for an attraction in Toy Story Land or on Sunset Blvd instead of Star Tours (which we would recommend) no worries. Typically Star Tours is a shorter wait than Toy Story or Slinky Dog.

Visit the Little Mermaid – If your children are in favor, this would be a good time to swing by the Voyage of the Little Mermaid in Animation Courtyard. The wait time is usually somewhat short. If your kids are indifferent, move on, there is so much more to see and do.

Disney Junior – After your voyage with the Mermaid, you may choose to head further into animation Courtyard for Disney Junior Live on Stage. If your kids have outgrown Disney Junior and you wish to take a pass on this show. Move on...

Star Wars Launch Bay – Further into Animation Courtyard is Star Wars Launch Bay. You can head there if you would like to meet the heroes and villains of the Star Wars Saga. This will be a big hit for most children.

Is Anyone Getting Hungry Yet?

READY. SET. DISNEY

Notes

DINNER

Below, we have chosen our top 3 dinner options for families with older children. Check out Section 2 earlier in this book for detailed descriptions of some of our favorite restaurants.

Our Favorite Dinner Options (Older children)

Counter Service	Sit-Down	Premium
Sunset Ranch Market	Mama Melrose	The Brown Derby
PizzeRizzo	50' Prime Time Café	
ABC Commissary	Hollywood and Vine	

We chose Sunset Ranch Market for families with older children because there is a huge variety of options there. Sunset Ranch is actually a food court of sorts, with a few different restaurants to choose from.

Also, it is located on Sunset Blvd just across from the next attraction on your Daily Guide Map – "Beauty and the Beast – Live on Stage." PizzeRizzo is good Pizza and free drink refills if you'd rather head there.

We chose Mama Melrose because the atmosphere and food are amazing. The 50's Prime Time Café is the next best option for a sit-down meal at Hollywood. The Sci Fi Diner is good and unique, but the old movies are nothing special.

The food at the Brown Derby is very good but it's very expensive and we prefer Mama Melrose. Also, The Derby will cost you 2 sit-down meal allowances if you are on the meal plan. Not worth it in our opinion.

READY, SET, DISNEY

Notes

EVENING

Beauty and the Beast or Lightning McQueen

If you have made it to this point, WAY TO GO!!! Our favorite night spot at Hollywood Studios is Sunset Blvd. There is always a ton going on here at night and the atmosphere is fun and lively.

At this point you might want to check your Times Guide to see when the next showing of _Beauty and Beast – Live on Stage_ is scheduled. You will want to be at least 20 to 30 minutes early for the show.

If you kids prefer you might rather choose to head over Lightning McQueen's Racing Academy. This will be especially attractive to the aspiring Race Car drivers in your family.

Twilight Zone Tower of Terror and Rock N Roller Coaster

Now it's time to use your Fast Pass, if you have one, for the Tower of Terror or Rock 'N' Rollercoaster. Ride the one you have a FP for and then wait in line for the other. If you have already used your FP in Tier 1 on another attraction you may choose to wait in line for both.

Note that the wait times usually decrease the last hour or two before park closing so you may want to wait if you have time later to return.

Snack It Up!

If you have acquired a "rumbly in your tumbly" (Pooh), consider grabbing a Sundae or Ice Cream Cookie Sandwich at Hollywood Scoops on the way by. This is one of our favorite snack locations at Hollywood Studios! We love it!

READY. SET. DISNEY

Rock 'n' Roller Coaster Tip - If you would like to ride the Rock 'N' Roller Coaster but the line is super long and you have no FP, consider splitting up and riding in the single rider line.

Top Secret Tip – If there is an attraction that you haven't been able to ride because Fast Passes were unavailable, and / or the lines were too long, there is a trick.

If you are able to stick it out until just before the park closes, get in line 5 minutes before park closing. When the park closes, all Fast Pass returns will end. The line for every ride is typically cut in half (at least). As long as you are in line before the park closes, you will not be turned away.

We have done this for many rides at Disney like: The Seven Dwarfs Mine Ride, Space Mountain, Avatar Flight of Passage, Frozen Ever After, Soarin, Test Track, Toy Story Mania, Rockin Roller Coaster and The Tower of Terror. It usually works really well.

<u>How To End the Evening</u> – Times vary throughout the year for <u>Fantasmic</u> and <u>Star Wars: A Galactic Spectacular</u>. If you would like to see both, it may be necessary for you to use one of your Fast Passes to reserve a spot for Fantasmic after the Firework show. If you must choose between the two, go with Star Wars...

May The Force Be With You...

Notes

READY, SET, DISNEY

NINTEEN

EPCOT

EPCOT: A QUICK OVERVIEW

Wanna Slow Down A Bit?

Epcot is a magical place that brings the entire World together in one park. Though much of its wonder and creative genius may only be appreciated by older visitors, there is plenty of magic for children at Epcot as well.

However, if you plan to hop from park to park a bit during your stay or want to spend a little down time at the pool, this might be a good day to try and fit that into your schedule.

We have outlined options in this Guide Map for families with younger children under 40" tall. However, many Epcot attractions appeal to all ages. We have also given some ideas for the older members of your family as well. Unless the park is super busy, a typical family can have an amazing time at Epcot in 5 hours or less.

Some families with younger children choose to bypass Epcot thinking it to be exclusively for the older crowd. However, some of the most exciting adventures at Disney for children, including some great character greeting opportunities, can only be experienced at Epcot.

READY. SET. DISNEY

Especially For Younger Children Under 40" Tall

Since you have younger children under 40" tall, we will suggest attractions best suited for them. The Seas with Nemo and Friends will be a huge hit for young children. They will enjoy Turtle Talk with Crush, The Nemo and Friends attraction and the indoor aquariums loaded with dolphins, sharks, sting rays and Nemo – of course.

We also recommend the Epcot Character Greeting Spot where they will meet Mickey, Minnie, Goofy and others. You will also want to get to Frozen Ever After in Norway, where you can meet Anna and Elsa, the interactive agent adventure with Perry the Platypus and The Grand Fiesta Tour starring the Three Caballeros in Mexico.

Especially For Older Children Over 40" Tall

If you also have older children in your family, there are several highlights that you will not want to miss. Your older children will especially enjoy Test Track, Soarin and Mission Space. Not that your older children wouldn't enjoy many of the same attractions that your younger children enjoy, they certainly will. There are some Disney attractions you just never outgrow.

Epcot Highlights

Spaceship Earth – Travel through time and grow in appreciation for the amazing progress and ingenuity of the human race. This educational adventure will be a big hit for the entire family.

The Seas With Nemo And Friends – This building is a wonderful adventure and celebration of life in the Sea. Regardless of age, there is something exciting for everyone.

Visit "The Seas with Nemo and Friends" attraction or get up close with a super righteous turtle in "Turtle in Turtle talk with Crush". Don't miss this under the Sea wonderland.

The Nemo And Friends Ride - Journey in a shell through the story of Finding Nemo. You can't help but sing along to this colorful animated adventure.

Turtle Talk With Crush – Spend some time hanging out with Crush from Finding Nemo. This attraction is sure to make a "splash" with the younger members of your family.

Living With The Land – Living with the Land is a wonderful educational experience for adults and children of all ages. Take a boat ride and discover the many imaginative ways that Disney is learning to live with the land. If you get to The Land, be sure to make time for this attraction too. We really enjoy it.

.

READY. SET. DISNEY

Test Track - This is another one of our favorites. Design your own car and see how it performs against other designs out on the open road. I usually go for power over efficiency but, to each his (or her) own. Its fast and fun!

Soarin – Catch the wind and Soar over several of the world's most iconic sights. This is an exhilarating panoramic journey that you absolutely must include in your Epcot experience if possible.

Mission Space – Blast off to outer space on a nine -month journey to Mars. You are guaranteed to encounter some major G's on this ride. If you are prone to motion sickness you might want to take a pass.

Frozen Ever After – Join Anna, Elsa, Olaf and others in this Frozen boat ride sing along. The kids will love it. I would guess that you will have fun too.

Agent P's World Showcase Adventure. A fantastic way for your children to experience the World Showcase is to send them on a top-secret mission with Perry the Platypus to defeat Dr Doofenshmirtz. Your family will be led to key locations throughout the World Showcase to uncover secret clues. You will need to download the "Play at Disney Parks" app on your phone to enjoy this attraction.

There are several missions to choose from so you can go on a mission in several different countries if you choose. This has been an Epcot highlight for each of our girls throughout their younger years.

The Disney and Pixar Short Film Festival – While wandering through Future World West, you may want stop at the Disney and Pixar Short Film Festival. This attraction is a tribute to some of the great films created by Disney and Pixar Films over the years. If you have young children, even if you don't, this attraction is worth seeing. For Disney film fans, it will be a humorous and nostalgic experience.

Gran Fiesta Tour Starring The Three Caballeros Join Donald Duck and the three Caballeros in this whimsical boat ride through Mexico. The ride combines the sights and sounds of Mexico with a relaxing, air conditioned and joy filled boat ride.

Films Of The Nations - You may also want to set aside some time in your schedule to check out the short films in China, America, France and Canada. Each of these films are beautiful and educational representations of their respective nations. The 360-degree circle film in Canada is especially impressive and has recently been updated and improved.

Shows And Entertainment – There are also shows that take place from time to time within many of the countries in the World Showcase. Check the Times Guide at the park on the day you arrive for show times. Some of these shows are random and show times may be unlisted.

Live Concerts – The concerts that occur nightly at Epcot in the World Showcase are always a highlight. We have heard great bands in Canada, The UK, Morocco, and America. Once again, check show times when you enter the park.

READY. SET. DISNEY

Epcot Forever – The new Laser and fireworks show at Epcot, Epcot Forever, is a fantastic way to end your evening at the park. The show, in our opinion, is a step up from Illuminations (the former nighttime show at Epcot). Epcot Forever incorporates many of the same firework displays as Illumination but with several surprising additions. You'll love it!

Make Your Fast Pass Reservations

In preparation for your Epcot day, we recommend that you book your Fast Passes as early as possible. The Fast Pass for <u>Frozen Ever After</u> will be the most difficult to get so try to book the FP for this ride first.

If you are staying at a Disney Resort, you will be able to make Fast Pass reservations 60 days before your arrival date. This is another incentive Disney offers to persuade visitors to stay on Disney property.

We recommend that you download the My Disney Experience App to make your FP reservations. Otherwise you can call Disney customer service directly at 407.939.1284. If you wish to make Fast Pass reservations to coincide with this Guide Map, we recommend that you make the following Fast Pass reservations for your day at Epcot:

<u>Morning Arrival (Young Children)</u>
Turtle Talk with Crush @ 9:00 am
Meet Mickey, Minnie and Goofy @ 11 am
Frozen Ever After @ 2 pm or later
Spaceship Earth (If Frozen is unavailable)

Morning Arrival (Older Children)
Test Track @ 9:00 am
Mission Space @ 11 am
Frozen Ever After @ 2 pm or later
Spaceship Earth (If Frozen is unavailable)

Afternoon Arrival (Young Children)
Turtle Talk with Crush @ 1 pm
Meet Mickey, Minnie and Goofy @ 2 pm
Frozen Ever After @ 4 pm or later
Spaceship Earth (If Frozen is unavailable)

Afternoon Arrival (Older Children)
Test Track @ 1 pm
Mission Space @ 2 pm
Frozen Ever After @ 4 pm or later
Spaceship Earth (If Frozen is unavailable)

Evening Arrival (Young Children)
Turtle Talk with Crush @ 4 pm
Meet Mickey, Minnie and Goofy @ 5 pm
Frozen Ever After 7 pm or later
Spaceship Earth (If Frozen is unavailable

Evening Arrival (Older Children)
Test Track @ 4 pm
Mission Space @ 5 pm
Frozen Ever After 7 pm or later
Spaceship Earth (If Frozen is unavailable

Take Advantage of the Child Swap – Since you have small children who are unable to visit the larger attractions, mom and dad can use a child swap for Soarin , Test Track, and Mission Space. These rides are super fun and will be highlights of your day at Epcot.

READY. SET. DISNEY

The child swap will allow both parents to ride with up to 2 kids while only one parent waits in line. The parent staying with the smaller children can head to another ride or grab a snack with the little ones. Got a FP, no one waits long, it's a great deal.

Fast Pass Rules – Again, you can check in to use your Fast Passes 5 minutes before your start time and up to 75 minutes after your start time. In other words, your Fast Passes are good for an hour from your start time, but they will still let you in up to 15 minutes after the hour is up. If you miss your Fast Pass altogether, ask for mercy. Sometimes the attendants will allow you to ride anyway.

Make Your Dining Reservations

The meal reservations that you make for this day will depend on your preference, whether you have the meal plan and your allotted budget. Epcot is loaded with options to fit just about any appetite. Each country offers food options that reflect the flavors of that country. You literally have the foods of the World offered in one magical place.

You are permitted to make meal reservations up to 6 months prior to your arrival date. To coordinate with this Guide Map, consider making one or more of the following meal reservation suggestions:

Our Breakfast Suggestions:

> <u>Breakfast</u> – Princess Storybook @ Akershusor Chip n' Dale's Harvest Feast
>
> <u>Lunch</u> – Princess Storybook Dining @ Akershus or Coral Reef
>
> <u>Dinner</u> – Via Napoli, Coral Reef or Princess Storybook

Most of the sit-down meal options in the World Showcase will require an advance reservation so we recommend that you choose early and make your reservations. If you change your mind, you can always cancel your reservation before midnight by the night before the reservation is scheduled.

We recommend that you make meal reservations to coordinate with the suggested FP time selections in your Guide Map if possible.

READY. SET. DISNEY

DISNEY
DAILY GUIDE MAPS

Epcot

READY. SET. DISNEY

EARLY MORNING

Deciding How To Spend Your Day - The way you spend your Epcot day will depend on the length of time you plan to spend at the park, your hopper plans and your energy level to this point in your vacation. We have given 3 arrival options to choose from (Early Morning, Afternoon and Early Evening).

If you choose Afternoon or Early Evening arrival, you may want to spend the morning relaxing by the pool or doing one of the free activities that we outline in Section 1 earlier in this book. If you plan on getting up early and hitting the ground running, maybe a quick breakfast at your resort or some granola bars on the go will do just fine.

Breakfast Anyone? – If you decide that you would like to kick start your day with an amazing breakfast, may we suggest that you make breakfast reservations at Princess Storybook in Norway. Princess Storybook would be a great way to begin your day at Epcot. Princess Storybook is also open for lunch or dinner if you prefer.

Photo Opportunity – As with other parks, if you arrive before or at park opening, you will likely be greeted by characters as you enter the park. This may be a great opportunity for a quick photo.

Where To Begin – We often prefer to begin our Epcot day at The Seas with Nemo and Friends in Future World West – If you plan to arrive early, we suggest that you either ride Spaceship

Earth as you enter the park or bypass Spaceship Earth and head straight for Future World West.

Head to the Seas with Nemo and Friends where you will use your FP for Turtle Talk with Crush, visit the Nemo and Friends attraction and explore the aquarium. This is a wonderful adventure for all young children. Parents tend to love it too.

READY. SET. DISNEY

Notes

LATE MORNING

The Land – Following your deep-sea adventures head over to The Land. At The Land, you could either check out <u>Living with the Land</u> or use a child swap and ride <u>Soarin (or both)</u>. The wait time for soaring may be a bit long without a FP.

Check for wait times on your My Disney Experience App. While in Future World West you may want to visit the <u>Disney and Pixar Short Film Festival</u>. This will be a big hit for the younger children

Visit Mickey and Minnie At The Character Greeting Spot – Before Leaving Future World West, be sure to use your FP to visit <u>Mickey, Minnie and Goofy</u>. While at the Epcot Character Greeting Spot you may have the opportunity to meet several other Disney characters as well.

Arriving Late To Epcot? – If you are planning a later arrival to Epcot, simply follow the same pattern latter in the day. Wait times will grow as the day progresses.

However, wait times for rides appealing to little ones are not affected as much as Soarin and Test Track. Frozen Ever After is typically always a long wait.

Top Secret Tip Concerning Epcot Crowds: Disney offers an Epcot annual pass that allows passholders to visit Epcot during the evenings only. This is one reason why Epcot is often busier in the evenings. If you wish to avoid the crowds, you might consider visiting Epcot earlier in the day and then hopping to another park just before or after dinner.

READY. SET. DISNEY

Future World East…Maybe? – If you have time to visit Future World East before lunch and have planned ahead and have gotten a FP for <u>Test Track</u>. This may be a good time to use the child swap and hop in a race car.

<u>Mission Space</u> is also a great ride if you want to give the older members of your party a quick thrill. Typically, the wait times for Mission Space are tolerable. Warning: The orange side is a bit more intense than the green.

Top Secret Tip For Little Ones: There are several options to keep the little ones occupied while waiting your turn to ride during a child swap. We love the exhibits in <u>Innoventions</u> and the free soda samples at <u>Club Cool</u>. For the littler ones, <u>Image Works</u> is a really nice interactive play area. This can actually be a good chance for one parent to spend some quality time with a younger child.

Notes

READY. SET. DISNEY

LUNCH TIME

Still Stuffed? – If you have chosen to stuff yourself for breakfast and want to eat a lighter lunch or just grab a snack, we recommend <u>The Sunshine Season's Grill</u> at The Land for a great variety of options.

There also great lunch options throughout the World Showcase. You can check the dining section in Section 2 of this book for a more detailed discussion of Epcot dining options

Character Dining Option – Below, we have chosen our top 3 lunch options. We have included our favorite choices for families with young children, families with older children and for adults. "*" denotes character dining experience.

<u>Princess Storybook Dining</u> is our choice for the best princess character dining at Disney because the food is really good, and you can meet the princesses without all the crowd stress of the Magic Kingdom.

Our Favorite Lunch Options (young children)

Counter	Sit-Down
Sunshine Seasons	Princess Storybook *
Electric Umbrella	Coral Reef
France - The Patisserie	Via Napoli
Norway – Kringla Bakery.	Mexico – La Cantina

Our Favorite Lunch Options (older children)

Counter	Sit-Down
Sunshine Seasons	Princess Storybook *
Electric Umbrella	Coral Reef
Norway – Kringla Bakery	Via Napoli
Mexico – La Cantina	

Our Favorite Lunch Options (adults)

Counter	Sit-Down	Premium
Sunshine Seasons	Via Napoli	La Cellier
Mexico – La Cantina	The Biergarten	
Japan – Katsura Grill		
UK – Yorkshire Co Fish Shop		
France - The Patisserie		

Explaining Our Picks – For younger and older children we often recommend the Sunshine Seasons Grill because of the great number of options available to picky eaters. Though their good options for adults as well, older children and adults may choose one of the "more sophisticated" options in the World Showcase.

The Coral Reef has pretty good food, but the real appeal is eating inside of the aquarium with sharks and dolphins. Again, Sunshine Season's in The Land is loaded with counter service options.

Endless Counter Service Options In The World Showcase. Here are a few of our favorites counter service choices. The Kringla Bakery in Norway has very good sandwiches and some of our favorite desserts.

The Patisserie in France has a great variety of delicious pastries and ala carte lunch items. We recommend the ham and cheese croissant – it's melt in your mouth good. The Brats at Sommerfest in Germany are always a great option.

The Yorkshire Co Fish Shop has really good fish and chips if you are up for something deep fried. If you enjoy sushi, The Katsura Grill in Japan would be a great option. Plus, the outside environment at Katsura is super beautiful. The tacos at La Cantina De San Angel are also a family favorite. Grab a table by the lake and enjoy the beautiful setting.

READY. SET. DISNEY

Great Sit-Down Meal Option In The World Showcase for lunch or dinner, we recommend <u>Via Napoli</u>. It has a unique Italian atmosphere with fantastic Italian cuisine. The kids will love the wood fired pizzas and lively atmosphere. If you like German food, the <u>Biergarten</u> has a friendly atmosphere with great German food.

The <u>San Angel</u> Restaurant in Mexico is also a family favorite with a wonderful Mexican environment. The Character dining at Akershaus (<u>Princess Storybook</u>) is also a great option, especially if there are little princesses in your family. We consider Princess Storybook one of the best Character Dining Experiences at Disney.

Secret Tip regarding Via Napoli – Although Via Napoli is usually booked solid if you attempt to make a same day reservation on the My Disney Experience app, no worries. On several occasions we have gone to the front desk and asked for availability. Usually they can fit you in if you are willing to come back an hour or so later. Via Napoli is a super fun environment loved by most kids and adults alike.

Notes

READY. SET. DISNEY

AFTERNOON

Some Hopper Options – Since visitors can travel from Epcot to Hollywood Studios by boat and to The Magic Kingdom by Monorail, it is fairly easy to hop to to from Epcot to the other parks (Animal Kingdom excluded).

Hop To Epcot – Therefore, you may choose to get an early start at another park and ride all the rides you can before the park gets super busy. Then you can hop over to Epcot and follow this Guide Map.

Hop From Epcot - Another option would be to arrive early at Epcot and shoot over to The Magic Kingdom or Hollywood Studios later in the day to catch the Fireworks Show.

Either way, you should be able to maximize your Fast Passes at Epcot while taking advantage of a few of your favorite attractions at another park earlier (or later) in the day.

Visit The Board Walk - If you would like a change of pace, we highly recommend that you "take a walk on The Boardwalk".

Toward the back of the World Showcase between France and The United Kingdom there is an Epcot exit that will lead you on a picturesque excursion onto Disney's Boardwalk. This is a beautiful walk and it may add just a little more magic to your already magical day.

The Boardwalk is packed with restaurants, shops, bakeries, street vendors and beautiful lake views. This might be a great opportunity to grab an ice cream cone or a cold beverage and relax on a quiet bench.

Find A Quiet Place To sit and unwind – There are also many quiet places to sit and unwind inside of Epcot. One of our favorite places to sit and relax is at the eating area of the Katsura Grill in Japan – It is beautiful and tranquil.

We also love sitting on the back streets in France, on the water in Mexico or in the open area on the streets of Italy. There is also a good place on the water in the UK behind the Rose and Crown.

Exploring And Discovery – Traveling to Hollywood Studios from Epcot by boat is a fantastic way to see a part of Disney World that many people never get to see.

If you need a break and feel a little adventurous, why not jump on a boat and take the ride to Hollywood Studios and back. You don't even need to enter Hollywood Studios unless you want to hop there for the evening. Regardless, the boat ride is an adventure in itself.

READY. SET. DISNEY

Notes

LATE AFTERNOON

Use Your FP for Frozen Ever After – After an early afternoon break, it's time to use your fast Pass to ride Frozen Ever After and then visit Anna and Elsa at Royal Sommerhus.

If your FP is not available yet, you could head to Mexico and take the Gran Fiesta Tour Starring the Three Caballeros.

Don't Pass On Perry – Though you may be tempted at this point to pass on your mission with Perry the Platypus, we strongly encourage you to press on.

The mission or missions that your young ones take with Perry will likely be the highlight of their day at Epcot. So many miss this experience at Epcot, not realizing how awesome it is.

So, head to Disney's Phineas and Ferb: Agent P's World Showcase Adventure at the entrance the World Showcase and help prevent Dr Doofenshmirtz from taking over "the entire Tri-state area." You will be so glad that you did.

Explore the World - After helping Perry rescue the Tri-State area, or in this case, the World Showcase, there are several options depending on your energy level. The World Showcase is an amazing display of architecture from around the World. Though you could spend hours in each country, don't leave Epcot without at least taking a brief tour of the nations around the World Showcase.

Some Endless Options In The World Showcase There are shows, concerts, Circle-Vision movies, boat rides and much more to see in the Showcase. It's a fabulous cultural experience. If you have a snack urge, sweet or savory, there are

READY, SET, DISNEY

options in every country to choose from. Maybe have each family member choose a dessert from one of the countries and then share them – that's what we do…

Notes

READY. SET. DISNEY

DINNER

Below, we have chosen our top 3 dinner options for families with younger children. It's very hard to choose food options at Epcot because there are so many to choose from. We recommend, if you have a favorite food type or would like to try food options from a certain nation, go for it.

Share Foods From The World Showcase – We often split up, grab food from different countries and meet somewhere to eat our meals together.

At Epcot it's hard to go wrong. "*" denotes character dining. Check out Section 2 earlier in this book for detailed descriptions of some of the better restaurants.

Our Favorite Dinner Options (Young Children)

Counter Service	Sit-Down	Premium
Sunshine Seasons	Princess Storybook *	Le Cellier
Liberty Inn	Via Napoli	
World Showcase	Coral Reef	

Our Favorite Dinner Options (Older Children)

Counter Service	Sit-Down	Premium
Sunshine Seasons	Princess Storybook *	Le Cellier
Liberty Inn	Via Napoli	
Yorkshire Co Fish Shop	Coral Reef	

Our Favorite Dinner Options (Adults)

Counter Service	Sit-Down	Premium
La Cantina	Via Napoli	Le Cellier
Sunshine Seasons	San Angel	
Yorkshire Co Fish Shop	Rose & Crown	
Katsura Grill	Biergarten	

Many Meal Options – Though we have recommended a few of our favorites, your choice for dinner will depend on whether you are favoring the kids or the adults. Also, you may want to choose a restaurant based solely on curiosity or your favorite food type.

The meal options are plentiful at Epcot so choose an option that best fits your family. Once again, you can find a more detailed description of Epcot restaurant choices in the restaurant section of our book, **Ready. Set. Disney**

International Food Options - There are a variety of international food options available at Epcot that you may never have had the opportunity to experience. Epcot allows you the chance to step outside the box and experience a new flavor from another culture. Regardless of your restaurant choice, we are guessing you won't be disappointed.

READY. SET. DISNEY

Notes

EVENING

Epcot Forever - If you have made it to this point, WAY TO GO!!! Epcot is one of our favorite evening environments at Disney World. We love to walk around the World Showcase at night and watch Epcot Forever.

There are very few bad locations around the World Showcase to watch Epcot Forever, but we do have a few favorites

Where To Watch? – We love to eat a late dinner in Mexico at <u>La Cantina De San Angel</u> about an hour before Epcot Forever and stick around for the show.

Another great location to view Epcot Forever is across the lake in The UK at <u>The Rose and Crown.</u>

There are great views on the benches <u>between China and Germany</u> and at the umbrella tables across from <u>the Outpost</u>. Regardless, because the show is over the lake and the world borders the lake all the way around, it's pretty easy to find a good spot.

Don't Rush Out – After the firework show, it may pay to relax and enjoy the music for 10 to 15 minutes before heading for the exit. This will give time for the crowd to clear out.

Some of our favorite memories at Epcot involve walking around the World Showcase after the park has closed. The music is amazing, and the atmosphere is joyful and lively.

READY. SET. DISNEY

Top Secret Line Tip – If there is an attraction that you haven't been able to ride because Fast Passes were unavailable, and / or the lines were too long, there is a trick.

If you can stick it out until just before the park closes, get in line 5 minutes before the park closing. At this point all Fast Pass returns will end. The line for every ride is typically cut in half (at least). As long as you are in line before the park closes, you will not be turned away.

We have done this for many rides at Disney like: The Seven Dwarfs Mine Ride, Space Mountain, Avatar Flight of Passage, Frozen Ever After, Soarin, Test Track, Toy Story Mania, Rockin Roller Coaster and The Tower of Terror. It usually works really well.

Notes

TWENTY

ANIMAL KINGDOM

ANIMAL KINGDOM: A QUICK OVERVIEW

One Amazing Park -The Animal Kingdom is an amazing park with a ton to see and experience. Some choose to bypass the Animal Kingdom thinking it to be somewhat of a glorified zoo. We too had that idea before visiting the Animal Kingdom as well.

Our "it's just as zoo" misconceptions were corrected right away on our first visit to the park. Now the Animal Kingdom is a family favorite and often our first stop upon arriving at Disney World.

Not A Zoo – Missing out on the Animal Kingdom would be a huge mistake since it has an amazing atmosphere, some great rides, and, in our opinion, three of the best shows at Disney World - <u>The Festival of the Lion King</u>, <u>Finding Nemo The Musical and Up! A Great Bird Adventure.</u> The Animal Kingdom is also home to 2 of our favorite rides as well: <u>Expedition Everest</u> and <u>Avatar Flight of Passage.</u>

Don't Miss These Shows - There are several highlights that your family will not want to miss. First, the three shows mentioned above are excellent for all ages and will offer adults a couple relaxing air-conditioned breaks throughout the day.

READY. SET. DISNEY

The Animal Kingdom At Night – Evening is a very special time to enjoy the Animal Kingdom since the park has an "awakening" of sorts after the sun goes down. The <u>Rivers of Light Night-Time Spectacular</u> and <u>Tree of Life Awakenings</u> add to the Magic and wonder of the Animal Kingdom after dark. Also, the Land of Pandora is a night-time wonder that you absolutely should see if possible.

Also, Don't Miss These Attractions – The Kilimanjaro Safari, Avatar Flight of Passage, Expedition Everest, Kali River Rapids, Dinosaur, It's Tough To Be A Bug, Up, The Gorilla Exploration Trails and Maharajah Jungle Trek.

Where To Begin? – The Animal Kingdom has a lot to see and do. It's possible to spend a full day at the park and still not see and do everything. We have done our best to design a plan that will help your family make the most of your day at the Animal Kingdom Park.

Using This Guide Map - The Guide Map section beginning on page 17 will be especially helpful on the day that you attend the Animal Kingdom park. We recommend that you take some time to read through this Guide Map before you go, make notes in the notes sections and let the booklet help guide you step by step through the park.

SHOWS & SPECIAL FEATURES

The Lion King Show – In our opinion, there is no other show at Disney that tops The Lion King. The show is interactive, humorous and extremely entertaining. Led by the characters of the Lion King and a cast of talented acrobats, dancers and singers, this show is a must see for all ages.

Finding Nemo Show – Another incredibly entertaining show at the Animal Kingdom park is the Finding Nemo Show. The actors and singers in this show make the Finding Nemo story come alive in a whole new way. All ages will appreciate this magical Under the Sea adventure.

Up! A Great Bird Adventure Show – This is another great live action show at the Animal Kingdom park. Join Russell, Dug and a flock of exotic birds in this humorous actioned packed show. This show is entertaining, educational and full of laughs.

Rivers of Light Night-Time Spectacular – This is a magical display of color and light as a pageant of lantern floats and laser light technology combine to tell the story of the Animal Kingdom. We love to grab some popcorn, a hot drink and a blanket (if its chilly) and end the day with this magical show.

Tree Of Life Awakenings – After dark, the animals buried in the Tree of Life come alive. We love to grab a snack or a drink and watch the Tree awaken. Some great spots for viewing are in Africa or Asia directly across from the tree or at the entrance to Discovery Island.

READY. SET. DISNEY

RIDES AND ATTRACTIONS

The Kilimanjaro Safari – The Safari is a highlight for every visitor to the Animal Kingdom. The 25 to 30-minute excursion takes you throughout the heart of the African Savanah where you will get up close with tons of African animals like Lions, Rhinos, Zebras, Cheetahs, Hippos, Crocodiles, Giraffes and more. You will also get to ride in a really cool Safari truck. This is also a must see for all ages.

Avatar Flight of Passage – Fly on the back of a mountain Banshee during an exhilarating 3D ride above this vast moon. These are the words Disney uses to describe the Flight of Passage ride.

This ride is over the top good. You get the actual sensation of flying on a Banshee. You can actually feel the Banshee breathing as you ride. Definitely one of our favorite attractions at Disney

Expedition Everest – I don't know if there is a ride that we have enjoyed more over the last 10 years. This is a thrilling roller coaster themed around an expedition into the Himalayas to explore the existence of the fabled Yeti. Watch out, there is a good chance that you will discover the truth about the Yeti: He does exist after all!

Kali River Rapids – An action-packed ride through the turbulent waters of a jungle river. Chances are…you will get wet.

Dinosaur – Travel back in time to the era of the dinosaur. Encounter some friendly species and some not so friendly. Help save one species from extinction. Great ride...very loud.

It's Tough To Be A Bug – This 3D show features Flick and a myriad of insects putting on a show for the guests to The Animal Kingdom – "Honorary Bugs." This show is hilarious and a bit startling at times. Very little children may be a little too startled at a few points.

Exploration Trails – The Gorilla Falls Exploration Trail in Africa and The Jungle Trek in Asia are both fantastic excursions for all ages. Walk at your own pace and stay as long as you like. Get up close with Gorillas, Tigers, Hippos and more.

Wilderness Explorers - There are also several adventures that you may want to squeeze in depending on the age and interests of your kids.

Wilderness Explorers allows young adventurers to complete challenges and earn badges as you work your way around the park. Check your park map for starting locations throughout the park.

The Dino Dig Site - Another great option for the little ones is the dinosaur dig-site playground called The Boneyard. This is a wonderful playground and can serve as a brief break time for mom and dad. Maybe a good chance to grab a snack or cool drink and relax a bit.

READY. SET. DISNEY

MAKING FAST PASS RESERVATIONS

In preparation for your Animal Kingdom day, we recommend that you book your Fast Passes as early as possible. The Fast Pass for <u>Avatar Flight of Passage</u> will be the most difficult to get so book the FP for this ride first.

If you are staying at a Disney Resort, you will be able to make Fast Pass reservations <u>60 days before your arrival date.</u>

We recommend that you download the <u>My Disney Experience App</u> to make your FP reservations. Otherwise you can call Disney customer service directly at 407.939.1284.

If you wish to make Fast Pass reservations to coincide with this guide map, we recommend that you make the following Fast Pass reservations for your day at the Animal Kingdom:

Winter park hours will somewhat alter the FP times you choose since the park will often close a bit earlier.

FAMILIES WITH OLDER CHILDREN:

For Early Arrival
Kilimanjaro Safari @ 9
Expedition Everest @ 10 am
Avatar – Flight of Passage @ 11 am

For Afternoon Arrival
Expedition Everest @ 1 pm
Avatar – Flight of Passage @ 2 pm
Kilimanjaro Safari @ 6 or 7pm

For Early Evening Arrival
Expedition Everest @ 4 pm
Avatar I Flight of Passage @ 5 pm
Kilimanjaro Safari @ 6 or 7pm

FAMILIES WITH YOUNGER CHILDREN:

For Early arrival
UP @ 9 am
Finding Nemo – The Musical @ 10 am
Meet Minnie and Mickey @ 11 am

For Afternoon Arrival
UP @ 1 pm
Finding Nemo – The Musical @ 2 pm
Meet Minnie and Mickey @ 3 pm

For Early Evening Arrival
UP @ 4 pm
Finding Nemo – The Musical @ 5 pm
Meet Minnie and Mickey @ 6 pm

Seasonal Park Hours – Depending on the season and park hours, you may be able to adjust your Fast Passes a little later. If the park is open later on the night you attend, you could move the Safari closer to park closing. This would give you greater flexibility with some of the other attractions you would like to visit.

Fast Pass Rules – Again, you can check in to use your Fast Passes 5 minutes before your start time and up to 75 minutes after your start time.

In other words, your Fast Passes are good for an hour from your start time, but they will still let you in up to 15 minutes after the hour is up.

If you miss your Fast Pass altogether, ask for mercy. Sometimes the attendants will allow you to ride anyway.

READY. SET. DISNEY

Don't Forget The Child Swap – If mom and dad want to use a child swap and ride a couple of the best rides at Disney, we recommend <u>Expedition Everest</u> and <u>Avatar Flight of Passage.</u> If you don't mind getting wet, <u>Kali River Rapids</u> is a wonderful adventure as well.

How The Child Swap Works – Just go to the attendant at the entrance to the ride and ask for a Child Swap Pass. One parent waits in line with up to 2 older children. After riding, the other parent rides with the older children without waiting in line. This allows both parents the opportunity to ride with up to 2 kids while only one parent has to wait in line.

The parent staying with the smaller children can head to another ride or grab a snack with the little ones until it is their chance to ride. If you have Fast Passes for the ride, no one waits long, it's a great deal all the way around.

MAKING DINING RESERVATIONS

The meal reservations that you make for this day will depend on your preference, whether you have the meal plan and your allotted budget.

You are permitted to make meal reservations up to 6 months prior to your check in date. Later in the Guide Map section we give you dining suggestions. If you would like to coordinate with this Guide Map, consider making one or more of the following meal reservations:

<u>Breakfast</u> – The Boma @ The Animal Kingdom Lodge

<u>Lunch</u> – Donald's Safari Character Dining @ Tusker House

<u>Dinner</u> – The Boma @ The Animal Kingdom Lodge

We understand that it is unlikely that you will choose to eat at the Boma twice and at a character meal on the same day. That's a ton of food. Haha. Though I'm sure that some of you are up for the challenge, we only offer multiple meal suggestions to guide you in the various options from which you may choose.

Coordinate With The Guide Map When Possible - If your schedule permits, we recommend that you make meal reservations to coordinate with the suggested FP time selections in your Guide Map. We have made suggestions to coincide for both families with younger and older children, but you may choose a menu that favors the adults in your group if you prefer.

READY. SET. DISNEY

DISNEY
DAILY GUIDE MAPS

Animal Kingdom

READY. SET. DISNEY

EARLY MORNING

We suggest that you start your Animal Kingdom day by eating a quick breakfast in your room or a quick service meal at your resort or hotel. If you would like to delay your Animal Kingdom entrance until later in the day, this may be a good opportunity to take advantage of some of the free fun highlighted in Section 1 of this book.

Breakfast Anyone? - If you decide that you would like to kick start your day with an amazing breakfast, we suggest that you make breakfast reservations at the <u>Boma</u> at The Animal Kingdom Lodge.

The Lodge is a must see for those who can fit it in to their schedule and the Boma is one of our favorite restaurants to eat at while on the meal plan. If you prefer, you could end your day at the Boma instead. The dinner buffet options are even better.

It is very difficult to eat a buffet and still arrive at the Animal Kingdom early, so we recommend that if you decide to eat at a buffet or sleep in a bit, choose the later Fast Pass options provided in this Guide Map.

If you arrive before or at park opening, you will likely be greeted by Disney characters as you enter the park. This may be a great opportunity for a quick photo.

Early Arrival?

Begin With Kilimanjaro Safari - If you plan to arrive early, we suggest that you begin your day by using your first Fast Pass at the <u>Kilimanjaro Safari</u> followed by a walk through the <u>Gorilla Falls Exploration Trail</u> which is adjacent to the Safari.

The animals on the Safari are typically more active the first thing in the morning or later in the day just before sunset. Choosing to go on the Safari at one of these times will give you the best chance of seeing the animals in their most active state.

The Gorilla Falls Exploration Trail – This trail is a great place to get up close with some Gorillas, Hippos and wild African birds. You can walk at your own pace and spend as little or as much time as you like on the trail.

Late Arrival?

If you plan to come to Animal Kingdom later in the day, just move the Safari and Gorilla Falls Exploration Trail later in the day. The Safari is also a good option later in the day since the animals tend to become more active around dinner time.

Rafiki's Planet Watch – If you have time and would like to check out Rafiki's Planet Watch, this would be a good opportunity to do that. This will be especially attractive to very young children because there will be opportunities to pet the animals, but most older children will enjoy it as well.

READY. SET. DISNEY

Notes

LATE MORNING

Expedition Everest – After the Safari, (Or if you are just arriving to the park) head toward Asia to ride Expedition Everest. If you have chosen a FP for this ride you can use it now. Be careful, stories have been told of Yeti sightings high up in the Himalayan Mountains...

Expedition Everest Single Rider Line – If you want to ride Everest again and don't mind separating, jump into the single rider line. The wait time is typically only a few minutes for this line even when the lines are long.

Don't Miss Finding Nemo – After Everest, head over to Dinoland to watch <u>Finding Nemo – The Musical</u>. This show is great for all ages and will provide a relaxing and air-conditioned break to your day. Try to be at least 20 to 30 minutes early to make sure you get a seat.

Note: You may choose to go with a later Fast Pass time for Expedition Everest and go straight to <u>The Festival of the Lion King Show</u> while you are already in Africa.

The Festival of the Lion King is, in our opinion, the <u>best show at Disney</u>. We like to watch it a little later in the day but that's just a personal preference. Either way, both of these shows are "must-sees" so work them both into your schedule if possible.

Dinoland Explorations – After your Everest FP (or whichever FP you have chosen), if you have younger children you might consider exploring Dinoland a bit. The little ones will enjoy

READY. SET. DISNEY

riding <u>Tricera Top Spin</u> and playing around in the <u>Boneyard playground</u>. The older children may wish to head over to <u>Dinosaur</u> the ride for a super trip back into pre-historic times.

Notes

READY. SET. DISNEY

LUNCH TIME

Still Stuffed? – We suggest, if you choose to eat a large breakfast, that you consider skipping lunch or eating a lighter lunch at one of the counter-service options.

There is also a great snack place in Dinoland called Dino Bites that serves huge ice cream sandwich cookies and Sundaes.

Are You Starving? – If you have skipped breakfast and need a heartier meal for lunch, there are many restaurant options to fit your taste and budget at The Animal Kingdom.

Below, we have chosen our top 3 lunch options both for families with younger and older children. We have also given our choices for adults as well "*" denotes character dining experience.

Our Favorite Lunch Options (Younger Children)

Counter	Sit-Down	Premium
Satu'li Canteen	Donald's Safari *	
Pizzafari	Rainforest Café'	
Restaurantosaurus	Yak and Yeti	

Our Favorite Lunch Options (Older Children)

Counter	Sit-Down	Premium
Satu'li Canteen	Donald's Safari *	
Pizzafari	Rainforest Café'	
Restaurantosaurus	Yak and Yeti	

Our Favorite Lunch Options (Adults)

Counter	Sit-Down	Premium
Satu'li Canteen	Rainforest Cafe	
Pizzafari	Yak and Yeti	
Restaurantosaurus	Donald's Safari*	

Donald's Dining Safari At Tusker House is one of our favorite character dining experiences because it offers great food and a variety of characters with a little less stress than some of the other character dining experiences.

The Rainforest Café is located at the park entrance. This is a wild place to shop and eat. Your children will absolutely love it.

Secret Tip regarding The Rainforest Cafe - We recommend, if at all possible, that you make an effort to eat at The Rainforest Café while at The Animal Kingdom. The atmosphere is perfect for little ones though the occasional storm may frighten very little ones a bit.

If you plan ahead, you can go on to the Landry's Select website and sign up as a member. The membership will cost you $25 but you will get a $25 credit to use at the restaurant plus a $25 birthday credit.

Be sure to register your birthdate for the month you will be traveling to Disney. This will not likely coincide with your actual birthday month, but it doesn't matter, you can only pick one birthday month anyway. You will also get priority seating with your membership card. The wait time is typically not that long with or without the card and there is a nice area to shop and wait for "your safari to begin".

Disney Springs Rainforest And T-Rex – If you miss The Rainforest Café while at Animal Kingdom, you may also visit the one at Disney Springs. T-Rex is also a Landry Select restaurant at Disney Springs.

READY. SET. DISNEY

This is another great place for families. Be aware, wait times at Disney Springs are typically much longer than wait times at The Animal Kingdom. Having a Landry's Select membership card will expedite your seating and give you discounts on your meal. This is another great reason to get the Landry's Select membership card before you come.

Notes

READY. SET. DISNEY

AFTERNOON

Hopper And Relaxation Options – Since the Animal Kingdom is a bit of a hike from the rest of Disney, it doesn't make much sense to hop from The Animal Kingdom to another park unless you are not planning on returning to The Animal Kingdom.

Nevertheless, if you have your own transportation, hopping to another park for a bit might be more sensible.

Visit The Animal Kingdom Lodge - If you would like a change of pace, we highly recommend that you shoot over to the Animal Kingdom Lodge for a couple hours. The <u>Boma</u> is a great choice for breakfast, lunch or dinner.

There are viewing areas where you will see Giraffes, Zebras and other animals from the African Savanah. The Lodge is breathtaking and magical. If you have the proper apparel, the kids might consider cooling off in the beautifully themed African pool while you take an afternoon Siesta.

Find A Quiet Place To Sit And Unwind – One of our favorite places to sit and unwind is directly <u>across from the Tree of Life in Asia</u>. There are tables that overlook the tree with plenty of shade. There are also relaxing spots at the <u>Harambe Market</u> in Africa and the <u>Satu'li Canteen</u> in Pandora.

Exploring And Discovery – The Animal Kingdom has several walkways and trails that you may easily miss if you are not looking for them.

We absolutely love to explore the <u>trails on Discovery Island</u> around the Tree of Life. There are hundreds of animals carved into the tree. It may be fun for your little ones to see how many animals they are able to identify.

Another Hidden Gem - The short trails of the Oasis toward the entrance to the park. Most people just bypass these trails on the way in or out of the park. You won't regret taking a few minutes out of your day to explore these trails. There is so much to see that you might otherwise miss.

READY. SET. DISNEY

Notes

LATE AFTERNOON

Avatar Flight Of Passage – After an early afternoon break, it's time to use your FP for Avatar Flight of Passage. This ride is one of the very best at Disney and can be very difficult to get a FP for if you wait too long. If you were unable to get a Fast Pass for this attraction, see our secret tip later in this guide about getting in line as the park closes.

It's Tough To Be A Bug – There are a few attractions that you may want to hit if you have time before dinner. It's Tough To Be A Bug is a classic Animal Kingdom show that you will not want to miss. The wait time is typically less than 20 minutes so don't waste a Fast Pass on this one.

Secret Tip Regarding Shows At Disney: When you are going to see one of the larger shows at Disney don't be the first to enter the auditorium. Those who enter first have to file all the way across the row and get stuck on the far end. Instead, let a number of people in before you and you will be seated closer to the center of the auditorium.

Don't Miss The Festival Of The Lion King – We Mean it... If you haven't seen it yet, check the times for the Lion King Show and get going! You don't want to lose track of time and miss either this show or Finding Nemo. If you haven't seen both, head there now.

Kali River Rapids – Though this ride is likely to get you a little or a lot wet, it is a ton of fun. If it's hot and you want to cool off, go for it. Take along your poncho if you want to ride but prefer to stay dryer.

READY. SET. DISNEY

Don't Forget About The Safari – If you were a late arrival to the park, make sure that you get to The Kilimanjaro Safari within your allotted Fast Pass time. The evening is one of the best times to catch the animals out and active. Don't miss the Safari, it's awesome!

Na'vi River Journey - This a beautiful boat ride. Not as exciting as Avatar Flight of Passage but it's still pretty cool.

Maharajah Jungle Trek – This is a self-guided walk through the jungles of Southeast Asia. Along the way, you will see tigers, monkeys, bats and Komodo dragons.

Notes

READY. SET. DISNEY

DINNER

Below, we have chosen our top 3 dinner options for both families with younger and older children. We have also included our recommendations for adults as well "*" denotes character dining.

Our Favorite Dinner Options (Young Children)

Counter Service	Sit-Down	Premium
Satu'li Canteen	Donald's Safari *	
Pizzafari	Rainforest Café	
Restaurantosaurus	Boma	

Our Favorite Dinner Options (Older Children)

Counter Service	Sit-Down
Satu'li Canteen	Donald's Dining Safari*
Harambe Market	Boma or Rainforest Café
Flame Tree Barbeque	Yak and Yeti

Our Favorite Dinner Options (Adults)

Counter Service	Sit-Down
Satu'li Canteen	Boma
Harambe Market	Rainforest Café
Flame Tree Barbeque	Yak and Yeti

Explaining Our Picks – We recommend Donald's Dining Safari over The Rainforest Café and The Boma because children may prefer a character dining experience. Older children may prefer the Rainforest or Boma. Both options are super great. Our family (with older children) prefer the Rainforest or Boma. They are both super amazing choices. If you choose to eat at Donald's Dining Safari or The Boma, you will want to make dining reservations in advance.

Notes

READY. SET. DISNEY

EVENING

Pandora And Rivers Of Light - If you have made it to this point, WAY TO GO!!! Our two favorite night spots at the Animal Kingdom are <u>Pandora</u> – The World of Avatar and <u>Asia</u> – Rivers of Light.

Walking around in Pandora at night is a must if you can make it happen. Everything comes to life in Pandora after sunset. It is a magical world of light and wonder that will capture the imagination of every little one – if they are still awake. It is also a very romantic place to explore at night.

Rivers Of Light is a great way to end a wonderful day at the Animal Kingdom. We wouldn't want to hype this show up too much, but it is still something that everyone should see at least once.

If it is going to be a chilly evening, it wouldn't hurt to pack a blanket or two for the show. A fresh hot popcorn never hurts either.

Tree Of Life Awakenings - You may want to take some time before or after the Rivers of Light show to take in the magical display of animals coming to life on the Tree of Life. This can be a relaxing way to enjoy the end of the evening while waiting for the crowds to disperse before heading for the exit.

Top Secret Long Line Tip – If there is an attraction that you haven't been able to ride because Fast Passes were unavailable, and / or the lines were too long, there is a trick.

If you are able to stick it out until just before the park closes, get in line 5 minutes before the park closing. When the park closes, all Fast Pass returns will end. The line for every ride is typically cut in half (at least). As long as you are in line before the park closes, you will not be turned away.

We have done this for many rides at Disney like: The Seven Dwarfs Mine Ride, Space Mountain, Avatar Flight of Passage, Frozen Ever After, Soarin, Test Track, Toy Story Mania, Rockin Roller Coaster and The Tower of Terror. It usually works really well.

After Rivers Of Light - If you still have energy, you may choose to head over to the Animal Kingdom Resort if you haven't had the chance to visit during the day. The Animal Kingdom Lodge is even more romantic and beautiful at night. It would be well worth your time to take a detour to the lodge before heading back to your lodging for the evening.

Notes

READY. SET. DISNEY

Closing Thoughts

Is Disney The Secret To A Happy Family?

Having watched our girls grow up at Disney World over the past 21 years, it's a bit of an understatement to say that Disney contains many wonderful and happy memories for our family.

However, as much as we love Disney World and appreciate the countless memories that it has provided for our family, Disney does not hold the secret to a happy family.

Though Disney holds many happy memories, it is but one place among many that has given our family the opportunity to become closer and to bond with one another.

The truth is, the reason our family has enjoyed Disney World so much over the past 20 years has much more to do with all of the moments that we have spent loving each other during the long periods of time between each of our Disney vacations.

We have discovered that God is perfect family. A perfect love exists between the Father, the Son and the Holy Spirit. When we share in that perfect love, we are given the supernatural ability to love each other the way the Father, the Son and the Holy Spirit love each other. That's perfect love and perfect family.

Though it can be a wonderful place to show our love for one another, Disney is not "The Secret" to happiness within our families. A healthy loving family will not magically appear through the waving of the good fairy's magical wand or by wishing upon a star. God is Love and only He can bring true love and joy into a family.

Disney can be a place, one among many, where we can take the time to focus on and love those God has brought into our lives. It can be a magical place; it can be a place of wonder and faith. It can be a place where we teach our children that they are princesses and princes in the Kingdom of God, but without God working within our families, Disney is just another place.

May Disney become a place where you begin to enjoy the love of family within the love of God. I pray that your upcoming Disney trip is more than just another family vacation.

I pray that Disney World affords you the opportunity to invite God into your vacation, awakening in you a Celebration of life, a Celebration of the wonder in the world He has created and a Celebration of the gift of family that is modeled for us so beautifully in the Godhead...The Father, The Son, and The Holy Spirit.

Printed in Great Britain
by Amazon